SAT* Subject Test
U.S. History
Flashcards

Premium Edition with CD-ROM

Mark Bach

AP History Teacher
Seattle, Washington

Research & Education Association
Visit our website at
www.rea.com

Research & Education Association
61 Ethel Road West
Piscataway, New Jersey 08854
E-mail: info@rea.com

REA's Flashcard Book for the SAT U.S. History Subject Test Premium Edition with CD-ROM

Printed in the United States of America

ISBN 13: 978-0-7386-0705-4
ISBN 10: 0-7386-0705-3

L09-0101

About This Premium Edition with CD-ROM

REA's unique Premium Edition Flashcard Book features questions and answers to help you study for the SAT U.S. History Subject Test. This book, enhanced with an interactive CD-ROM, is designed to fit conveniently into your study schedule for SAT United States History. You'll find it's an especially effective study tool when paired with *REA's SAT Subject Test: U.S. History,* our celebrated comprehensive review and practice-exam book.

This handy volume is filled with 500 must-study SAT United States History questions and detailed answers. The book covers all the topics tested on the official exam, including the Colonial Period, the American Revolution, The Civil War and World War I. The full index makes it easy to look up a particular subject and review a specific historical time period.

Unlike most flashcards that come loose in a box, these flashcards are bound in an easy-to-use, organized book. This innovative Flashcard Book lets you write your answer to a question on the front of the card, and then compare it to the answer on the back of the card. REA's flashcards are a great way to boost your test-readiness and are perfect for studying on the go.

The interactive CD-ROM includes four test-readiness quizzes for you to take after studying the material in this book. The CD also includes timelines of all chronological periods covered on the SAT exam and a concise U.S. History review. Using all these materials will boost your confidence when you take the actual exam.

This Premium Edition Flashcard Book has been carefully developed with REA's customary concern for excellence. We believe you will find it an outstanding addition to your SAT United States History prep.

Larry B. Kling
Chief Editor

About the Author

Mark Bach has been teaching history courses since 1983 and is currently an online instructor at APEX Learning in Seattle, Washington. Mr. Bach received his B.A. in History, German and Religion from St. Olaf College in Minnesota and his M.A. from Michigan State University.

About Research & Education Association

Founded in 1959, Research & Education Association (REA) is dedicated to publishing the finest and most effective educational materials—including software, study guides, and test preps—for students in middle school, high school, college, graduate school, and beyond.

We invite you to visit us at *www.rea.com* to find out how "REA is making the world smarter."

Acknowledgments

In addition to our author, we would like to thank Larry B. Kling, Vice President, Editorial, for his overall guidance, which brought this publication to completion; Pam Weston, Vice President, Publishing, for setting the quality standards for production integrity and managing the publication to completion; John Cording, Vice President, Technology, for coordinating the design and development of REA's CD software; Diane Goldschmidt, Senior Editor, for editorial project management; Alice Leonard, Senior Editor, for preflight editorial review; Heena Patel, Technology Project Manager, for design contributions and software testing efforts; Christine Saul, Senior Graphic Designer, for designing our cover.

We also extend special thanks to Caroline Duffy and Marianne L'Abbate for copyediting, Hadassa Goldsmith for proofreading, and Kathy Caratozzolo of Caragraphics for typesetting this edition.

Questions

What was the Tennessee Valley Authority (TVA)? What did the TVA represent?

Your Answer _____

_____

What was the major consequence of World War I for blacks and other racial minorities?

Your Answer _____

_____

What was the "social gospel"?

Your Answer _____

_____

Correct Answers

A–1

1) The TVA, a public corporation under a three-member board, built twenty dams to stop flooding and soil erosion, improve navigation, and generate hydroelectric power.
2) The TVA represented the first major experiment in regional public planning.

A–2

About half a million rural southern blacks migrated to cities, mainly in the North and Midwest, to obtain employment in war and other industries, especially in steel and meat packing. Some blacks served in the U.S. Army and were decorated combat veterans.

A–3

The "social gospel" was a belief that Christianity could be the basis for better health and education services offered to the poor, many of whom were immigrants.

Questions

Q–4

What two major problems did immigrants face during the 1880s?

Your Answer _____

_____

Q–5

Who were the "copperheads" during the Civil War?

Your Answer _____

_____

Q–6

Why did Kansas become known as "Bleeding Kansas"?

Your Answer _____

_____

Correct Answers

A–4

Transitioning to a new culture and finding a place in the American economy.

A–5

Northerners opposed to the war with the South

A–6

Full-scale guerilla war erupted there after the election of two opposing territorial governments. The issue of whether to make Kansas a slave or free state resulted in localized violence.

Questions

Q–7

What immigrant group was the target of much job discrimination during the first half of the nineteenth century?

Your Answer _____

_____

Q–8

What are some of the explanations as to why the Salem witch trials occurred?

Your Answer _____

_____

Q–9

What was Bacon's Rebellion and what was its effect?

Your Answer _____

_____

Correct Answers

A–7

Irish Catholics

A–8

1) Religious differences between the members and nonmembers of the Congregational Church
2) Socioeconomic differences between the poorer farmers in the West and the wealthier merchants in the East

A–9

1) Nathaniel Bacon led a group of men, many of them former indentured servants, in burning Jamestown to show their disapproval of the colony's Indian policy.
2) It marked the turning point from the use of indentured servants to the use of African slave labor

Questions

Q–10

Why did the New England colonies enjoy widespread literacy?

Your Answer _____

_____

Q–11

What was the Manhattan Project?

Your Answer _____

_____

Q–12

What were three effects of the rise of the railroads in the 1840s and 1850s?

Your Answer _____

_____

Correct Answers

A–10

Puritans placed a great emphasis on reading because they believed that everyone should be able to read the Bible. Children were taught to read the Scriptures at a young age and to be able to write verses from the Bible.

A–11

The Manhattan Project was a top secret program during World War II. It was established in August 1942 for the purpose of developing an atomic bomb.

A–12

1) Big-business techniques spread.
2) A nationwide market developed.
3) The Midwest became linked to the North rather than to the South.

Questions

Q–13

What did the phrase "manifest destiny" mean?

Your Answer _____

_____

Q–14

Who were Industrial Workers of the World (aka the Wobblies)? Who was its leader? In what industries were they successful during the 1910s?

Your Answer _____

_____

Q–15

What were trusts?

Your Answer _____

_____

Correct Answers

A–13

Manifest destiny was a belief that it was the destiny of the United States to expand its territory over the whole North American continent.

A–14

1) The Wobblies were members of a radical labor organization.
2) "Mother" Mary Harris Jones
3) They had some success in the textile industry and western mining.

A–15

Corporate combinations and monopolies that manipulated prices

Questions

What was the Medicare Act of 1965?

Your Answer _____

_____

What was the consequence of the 1918 congressional elections on President Wilson's international stature?

Your Answer _____

_____

What was the Whiskey Rebellion? How did President George Washington respond to it?

Your Answer _____

_____

Correct Answers

A–16

The act combined hospital insurance for retired people with a voluntary plan to cover physician bills.

A–17

Wilson had appealed to the voters to elect a Democratic Congress, saying to do otherwise would be a repudiation of his leadership in European affairs. The voters gave the Republicans a slim margin in both houses in the election. This undermined Wilson's political support at home and his stature in the eyes of world leaders.

A–18

1) A group of Pennsylvania farmers refused to pay the excise tax on whiskey and also terrorized tax collectors.
2) President Washington sent 15,000 federal troops to crush the rebellion and to display the dominance of the federal government.

Questions

Q–19

In 1620, before going ashore, the Pilgrims drew up the _____ _____, which established an orderly government based on the consent of the governed.

Your Answer _____

Q–20

Who wrote *Uncle Tom's Cabin*? What effect did it have?

Your Answer _____

Q–21

What was the aim of the America First Committee?

Your Answer _____

Correct Answers

A–19

Mayflower Compact

A–20

1) Harriet Beecher Stowe wrote the book in the 1850's
2) It made many northerners active opponents of slavery and created sympathy for the North with the British public.

A–21

To keep America out of World War II

Questions

What were the effects of the Dred Scott decision?

Your Answer _____

_____

Why did Commodore Matthew Perry lead a U.S. naval force into Tokyo Bay in 1853?

Your Answer _____

_____

What was the Trail of Tears?

Your Answer _____

_____

Correct Answers

A–22

Many southerners were encouraged to take an extreme position on the slavery issue and to refuse any compromise. Many northerners were convinced that the decision was not final and that a pro-slavery conspiracy controlled the government.

A–23

To open Japan to American diplomacy and trade. Japan had isolated itself for over two hundred years after 1600.

A–24

The Trail of Tears was the forced march of thousands of Cherokees under army escort from Georgia to the West. Twenty-five percent or more of the Cherokees perished on this march.

Questions

Q–25

What well-known agricultural chemist studied at Tuskegee Institute?

Your Answer _____

_____

Q–26

The new continent discovered by Christopher Columbus in 1492 was named after _____ _____.

Your Answer _____

_____

Q–27

What was the theory behind supply-side economics advanced by the Republican party in the 1980's?

Your Answer _____

_____

Correct Answers

A–25

George Washington Carver

A–26

Amerigo Vespucci

A–27

If government left more money in the hands of the people, they would invest rather than spend the excess on consumer goods. The results would be greater production, more jobs, and greater prosperity.

Questions

Q–28

Who were the robber barons?

Your Answer _____

_____

Q–29

How were the members of the Electoral College elected prior to 1824?

Your Answer _____

_____

Q–30

How did the Virginia gentry respond to Britain's tightening of their local autonomy during the colonial era?

Your Answer _____

_____

Correct Answers

A–28

Powerful, often ruthless, capitalists who owed their wealth to exploitative business practices

A–29

By state legislatures

A–30

They used political means to block the governor's efforts to increase royal control.

Questions

Q–31

Who was the first and only president of the Confederate States of America?

Your Answer _____

_____

Q–32

What Soviet action prompted the Berlin Crisis in June 1948? How did the United States respond?

Your Answer _____

_____

Q–33

How did Bostonians react to Governor Thomas Hutchinson's plan to attempt to collect the tea tax? What was the British reaction to the colonists?

Your Answer _____

_____

Correct Answers

A–31

Jefferson Davis

A–32

1) The Soviets blocked surface access to Berlin.
2) The United States instituted an airlift to transport supplies to the city until the Soviets lifted their blockade in May 1949.

A–33

1) In the incident later called the Boston Tea Party, Boston colonists disguised themselves as Indians, boarded tea-bearing ships docked in Boston Harbor, and threw the tea overboard.
2) In response, the British passed the Boston Port Act, which closed Boston Harbor to all trade until Boston had paid for all the tea. In addition, any royal officials accused of crimes in Massachusetts would be tried elsewhere.

Questions

Q–34

Who were the *conquistadores*?

Your Answer _____

_____

Q–35

What did the Wright brothers invent?

Your Answer _____

_____

Q–36

Who was the first European to see the Pacific Ocean during the Age of Discovery?

Your Answer _____

_____

Correct Answers

A–34

Independent Spanish adventurers who led their country's army into the New World, seeking wealth, glory, and to spread the Roman Catholic faith

A–35

The airplane

A–36

Vasco Núñez de Balboa

Questions

Q-37

Describe President Herbert Hoover's economic philosophy.

Your Answer _____

_____

Q-38

Give one reason for the stock market crash of 1929 and the Great Depression that followed.

Your Answer _____

_____

Q-39

What new tax did the North impose in order to help finance the Civil War?

Your Answer _____

_____

Correct Answers

A–37

Hoover believed that an economic system with voluntary cooperation of business and government would enable the United States to abolish poverty through continued economic growth. He generally believed in non-intervention in the economy by the government.

A–38

Many people had bought stock on a margin of 10 percent, meaning that they had borrowed 90 percent of the purchase through a broker's loan and put up the stock as collateral. This led to overspeculation that created a "bubble" which burst in 1929.

A–39

The income tax was used temporarily to raise money for the war.

Questions

Q–40

What was the Fair Deal program?

Your Answer _____

_____

Q–41

Why did the New England colonists enjoy a more stable and well-ordered society than the Chesapeake Bay colonists?

Your Answer _____

_____

Q–42

What and who were indentured servants? What was the headright system?

Your Answer _____

_____

Correct Answers

A–40

The Fair Deal program embraced President Truman's proposals to enlarge and extend the New Deal. Some of its provisions included increasing the minimum wage, extending Social Security, and building more public housing.

A–41

Unlike the Chesapeake Bay colonists, New Englanders had migrated as family units and had a more stable and homogeneous population. New England had church congregations which acted as a foundation for many of the small communities in the area.

A–42

1) Indentured servants were people who exchanged their labor for passage to the New World during the early colonial era. Many times, these were sons who, due to primogeniture and the excessive labor supply in England, had few economic prospects at home.
2) The headright system gave grants of lands in the New World to those who paid the passage of indentured servants.

Questions

Q–43

What was Great Britain's first permanent settlement in the New World? What happened at this colony?

Your Answer _____

_____

Q–44

What was the SALT agreement of 1972?

Your Answer _____

_____

Q–45

During the Napoleonic Wars, American ships were seized by the French and the English, and American sailors were _____ into the British Navy.

Your Answer _____

_____

Correct Answers

A–43

1) Jamestown, Virginia
2) The colony suffered from disease due to the swampy environment where it was settled. Also, during the "starving time," many colonists died because many settlers were looking for wealth and not planting sufficient crops. The colony also suffered attacks from hostile Indians.

A–44

The Strategic Arms Limitation Treaty (SALT) was a treaty signed by the United States and the Soviet Union in 1972 in which both sides agreed to stop making ballistic missiles and to reduce the number of antiballistic missiles to 200 for each power.

A–45

impressed

Questions

Q–46

Why was the American victory at Saratoga, New York, in 1777, so important?

Your Answer _____

_____

Q–47

Why did the French manage to stay on relatively good terms with the Indians during the colonial period?

Your Answer _____

_____

Q–48

What were some actions taken by Theodore Roosevelt's administration with regard to conservation?

Your Answer _____

_____

Correct Answers

A–46

The American victory at Saratoga convinced the French to join openly in the war against England.

A–47

Relatively few Frenchmen came to America. Therefore, they were not infringing on Indian territories. Also, Frenchmen often married into tribes and learned native customs.

A–48

A number of national parks, forests, and irrigation projects were created; water power was developed; and the National Conservation Commission was set up to oversee the nation's natural resources.

Questions

Q–49

Who led the expedition to explore the western territory to the Pacific in 1804?

Your Answer _____

Q–50

The prevailing farming technique used in the first half of the nineteenth century was a _____ and _____ method that was wasteful of timber and diminished the fertility of the soil.

Your Answer _____

Q–51

What qualities did the Horatio Alger stories promote?

Your Answer _____

Correct Answers

A–49

Meriwether Lewis and William Clark

A–50

clearing and planting

A–51

Hard work and honesty

Questions

Q–52

Who wrote the pamphlet *Common Sense*? Why was it so important?

Your Answer _____

_____

Q–53

What is Rosa Parks famous for?

Your Answer _____

_____

Q–54

What civil rights measures did President Harry S. Truman enact in 1948?

Your Answer _____

_____

Correct Answers

A–52

1) Thomas Paine
2) It was widely sold and had a great deal of influence in urging Americans to achieve independence from Britain.

A–53

Rosa Parks's arrest on December 11, 1955, in Montgomery, Alabama, was a catalyst for the civil rights movement. She was arrested for refusing to give up her seat on a bus to a white passenger.

A–54

He banned racial discrimination in federal government hiring practices and ordered the desegregation of the armed forces.

Questions

Q–55

Describe how the Works Progress Administration (WPA) worked.

Your Answer _____

_____

Q–56

How did technology and urbanization lead to a sharp rise in the standard of living during the 1920s?

Your Answer _____

_____

Q–57

What was "yellow journalism" and why was it used?

Your Answer _____

_____

Correct Answers

A–55

The WPA employed people from the relief rolls for thirty hours of work a week at pay double the relief payment but less than private employment. Most of the projects undertaken were in construction.

A–56

Technological conveniences such as electric stoves, vacuum cleaners, refrigerators, washing machines, and toasters made life less burdensome. Urban living improved access to electricity, natural gas, telephones, and piped water.

A–57

1) Yellow journalism was a policy, followed by some newspapers, of sensationalizing the news, particularly exaggerating atrocities in Cuba.
2) It was used to increase circulation.

Questions

Q–58

What was Social Darwinism?

Your Answer _____

Q–59

True or False: The majority of southerners owned slaves.

Your Answer _____

Q–60

Who supported and opposed the temperance movement in nineteenth-century America?

Your Answer _____

Correct Answers

A–58

A philosophy of survival of the fittest projected into human affairs.

A–59

False. Three-fourths of the southern whites did not own any slaves.

A–60

Supported: Most Protestants
Opposed: New Catholic immigrants

Questions

Q–61

What was the major issue in the election of Andrew Jackson in 1832?

Your Answer _____

_____

Q–62

When was the Federal Reserve Act passed? What was the purpose of creating a new currency called Federal Reserve Notes? What mechanism was created to supervise the Federal Reserve System?

Your Answer _____

_____

Q–63

What major technological innovation in naval warfare took place during the Civil War?

Your Answer _____

_____

Correct Answers

A–61

The rechartering of the National Bank

A–62

1) The Federal Reserve Act was passed in 1913.
2) The currency was designed to expand and contract with the volume of business activity and borrowing.
3) The Federal Reserve Board was created to supervise the system.

A–63

The development of the ironclad ship replacing wooden hulls

Questions

Q–64

Who was Alexander Graham Bell?

Your Answer _____

_____

Q–65

According to the _____ _____ of 1819, Spain agreed to sell the remainder of Florida to the United States.

Your Answer _____

_____

Q–66

When was the United Nations formed? What countries are permanent members of the Security Council?

Your Answer _____

_____

Correct Answers

A–64

The inventor of the telephone

A–65

Adams-Otis Treaty

A–66

1) The United Nations was formed in 1945.
2) The United States, Great Britain, France, Russia (formerly the Soviet Union), and China are all permanent members.

Questions

How did the United States respond to the Soviet invasion of Afghanistan?

Your Answer _____

_____

When was D-Day? What did it signify?

Your Answer _____

_____

Why did prices in the South skyrocket during the Civil War?

Your Answer _____

_____

Correct Answers

A–67

The Carter administration stopped shipments of grain to the Soviet Union, withdrew SALT II from the Senate, and withdrew the United States from the 1980 Moscow Olympics.

A–68

1) June 6, 1944
2) D-Day signified the beginning of the liberation of Europe by the Allied forces.

A–69

Goods were in short supply, and the South issued so much paper money that it became practically worthless.

Questions

Q–70

What message was conveyed to European powers in the Monroe Doctrine?

Your Answer _____

_____

Q–71

What was the term used to describe the legislation passed between 1933 and 1935?

Your Answer _____

_____

Q–72

Why did Reconstruction end?

Your Answer _____

_____

Correct Answers

A–70

The Western Hemisphere was closed to future colonization by European powers.

A–71

The First New Deal

A–72

The North lost interest as a result of government corruption, a depression, general weariness about the difficulty of remaking southern society, and the death of Radical Reconstruction leaders. The presidential election of 1876 also hastened the end of the military occupation of the South.

Questions

Q–73

What were the Kentucky and Virginia Resolves?

Your Answer _____

_____

Q–74

What was the class origin of the women's movement?

Your Answer _____

_____

Q–75

What was the political tendency of the "Sunbelt" states since the 1980s?

Your Answer _____

_____

Correct Answers

A–73

These were a series of resolves in reaction to policies by President John Adams drawn up by Thomas Jefferson and James Madison. The resolves were presented to the Kentucky and Virginia legislatures; they proposed that John Locke's compact theory should be applied, thus nullifying federal laws in those states.

A–74

The women's movement was largely limited to the middle class.

A–75

Conservative

Questions

Q–76

What explains the growth of organized crime during the 1920s?

Your Answer _____

_____

Q–77

When did the importation of slaves from abroad become illegal?

Your Answer _____

_____

Q–78

Who was Mark Twain?

Your Answer _____

_____

Correct Answers

A–76

Prohibition, because organized crime helped meet the demand for illegal alcohol and made huge profits

A–77

1808

A–78

Mark Twain was a famous author of the late nineteenth to early twentieth century whose works include *The Adventures of Tom Sawyer* and *The Gilded Age.*

Questions

Q–79

What effect did the Republican split between Taft and Roosevelt have on the 1912 presidential election?

Your Answer _____

_____

Q–80

What was the "Crime of '73"?

Your Answer _____

_____

Q–81

What did the Child Labor Act of 1916 do? Why was the law especially significant? What happened to the law in 1918?

Your Answer _____

_____

Correct Answers

A–79

The split paved the way for a Democratic victory.

A–80

The demonetization of silver

A–81

1) The Child Labor Act of 1916 forbade shipment in interstate commerce of products whose production involved the labor of children under fourteen or sixteen, depending on the product.
2) The law was especially significant because it was the first time that Congress regulated labor within a state using the interstate commerce power.
3) The law was declared unconstitutional by the Supreme Court in 1918 on the grounds that it interfered with the powers of the states.

Questions

Q–82

How did President Rutherford B. Hayes respond to the railroad strike of 1877?

Your Answer _____

Q–83

Who helped develop the modern steel industry in the United States?

Your Answer _____

Q–84

What are "greenbacks"? Why do creditors/business-people dislike them, and why do debtors favor them?

Your Answer _____

Correct Answers

A–82

He used federal troops to restore order after numerous strikers were killed.

A–83

Andrew Carnegie

A–84

1) A currency not backed by specie first issued in 1862.
2) Creditors/businesspeople dislike them and debtors favor them because "greenbacks" cause inflation, which decreases the value of the money. So, debtors can pay off debt in money that is less valuable than the gold they borrowed.

Questions

In the second quarter of the nineteenth century, the South had an _____ economy.

Your Answer _____

What product replaced water as a major source of industrial power in the 19th century?

Your Answer _____

When was the Watergate break-in? What happened at the break-in?

Your Answer _____

Correct Answers

A–85

agrarian

A–86

Coal

A–87

1) June 17, 1972
2) Four men associated with President Nixon's re-election campaign broke into Democratic headquarters at the Watergate office-apartment complex. They were caught going through files and installing eavesdropping devices. Their arrest led to investigations that revealed abuses of power in the White House and finally resulted in the first resignation by a sitting president in American history.

Questions

Q–88

In the election of 1912, what was the term used to describe Democratic nominee Woodrow Wilson's platform? What were two features of this platform?

Your Answer _____

_____

Q–89

What was the "Freeport Doctrine"?

Your Answer _____

_____

Q–90

Why did the admission of Missouri in 1819 result in a controversy between the northern and southern members of Congress? How was this resolved?

Your Answer _____

_____

Correct Answers

A–88

1) Wilson's platform was called the New Freedom.
2) Two features of the platform were to restore economic competition through the breakup of monopolies and to lower tariffs.

A–89

The "Freeport Doctrine" was an argument by Senator Douglas in one of his debates with Abraham Lincoln. He argued that a territory could get around the *Dred Scott* decision by not passing the special laws that slave jurisdictions usually passed to support slavery.

A–90

Missouri's admission would upset the sectional balance in the Senate. As a compromise, Maine was admitted as a free state, Missouri was admitted as a slave state, and slavery was prohibited north of the 36°30′N latitude line in the Louisiana Territory.

Questions

Q–91

Why was the Act of Religious Toleration approved in Maryland?

Your Answer _____

_____

Q–92

What did the Indian Reorganization Act of 1934 do?

Your Answer _____

_____

Q–93

What two events contributed to the American declaration of war against Germany during World War I?

Your Answer _____

_____

Correct Answers

A–91

The Act of Religious Toleration was intended to protect the Catholic minority by granting freedom of worship to all Christian persuasions.

A–92

The Indian Reorganization Act restored tribal ownership of lands, recognized tribal constitutions and government, and provided loans to tribes for economic development.

A–93

1) Unlimited submarine warfare: Germany announced on January 31, 1917, that it would sink all ships, without warning, in a large war zone off the coasts of the Allied nations in the eastern Atlantic and Mediterranean.
2) The Zimmerman telegram: The British intercepted a secret message from the German foreign secretary, Arthur Zimmerman, to the German minister in Mexico in which the Germans proposed that, in the event of war between the United States and Germany, Mexico would attack the United States. When the telegram was released to the press on March 1, 1917, many Americans became convinced that war with Germany was necessary.

Questions

Q–94

What did President Theodore Roosevelt hope to accomplish by sending the great white naval fleet to Asian ports?

Your Answer _____

_____

Q–95

What were two reasons why many southerners believed that Great Britain and France would intervene on the Confederacy's behalf?

Your Answer _____

_____

Q–96

What were the Coercive Acts?

Your Answer _____

_____

Correct Answers

A–94

Roosevelt hoped to show American strength to China and Japan.

A–95

1) Great Britain and France would be happy to see a divided and weakened America.
2) British and French factories needed cotton from the American South.

A–96

The Coercive Acts were Britain's response to the dumping of tea by colonists in Boston Harbor.

Questions

Q–97

What was the Protestant Reformation?

Your Answer _____

_____

Q–98

In what industry was the moving assembly line first introduced?

Your Answer _____

_____

Q–99

Prior to the advent of the railroad, which commercial transportation system dominated domestic trade?

Your Answer _____

_____

Correct Answers

A–97

A religious movement begun by Martin Luther, who taught that an individual's salvation was determined by faith alone, rather than the church's elaborate sacraments overseen by the priesthood. This led to a division of Europe North and South between Protestants and Catholics.

A–98

The moving assembly line was introduced in the automobile industry by Henry Ford in 1913 and 1914.

A–99

Coastal sailing ships

Questions

Q–100

What was the Second Great Awakening?

Your Answer _____

_____

Q–101

What was Shays' Rebellion?

Your Answer _____

_____

Q–102

Why was the Boston Massacre labeled as such by Samuel Adams when only five people were killed and it was partially incited by the colonists?

Your Answer _____

_____

Correct Answers

A–100

The Second Great Awakening was a revival that took place in the beginning of the 1800s. Women and blacks were heavily involved in the movement, and it sparked the reforms of the 1830s and 1840s.

A–101

After America gained its independence from Great Britain, there was an economic depression. Daniel Shays led a group of New England farmers to shut down the Massachusetts courts so that the judges would not be able to seize property or condemn people to debtors' prisons for not paying taxes.

A–102

Adams wanted to incite the colonists to rise up against the British.

Questions

Q–103

Why did Spain and Portugal decide to draw up the Treaty of Tordesillas in 1493?

Your Answer _____

_____

Q–104

Why were skilled artisans less important in the factories of the Industrial Revolution?

Your Answer _____

_____

Q–105

What were the Lincoln-Douglas debates in 1858?

Your Answer _____

_____

Correct Answers

A–103

Spain wanted to confirm its ownership of New World lands but feared interference from Portugal, a powerful seafaring nation that had been active in overseas exploration.

A–104

Repetitive processes could be performed by relatively unskilled workers.

A–105

They were a series of seven debates held between Illinois Senator Stephen Douglas, who argued that popular sovereignty should dictate the slavery issue, and his electoral opponent, Abraham Lincoln, who argued that slavery was a moral wrong.

Questions

Q–106

During the Jacksonian era, why did northeasterners oppose the government's disposal of lands at cheap prices?

Your Answer _____

_____

Q–107

Thomas Jefferson and James Madison, who opposed Alexander Hamilton's Bank of the United States, came to be known as _____ _____.

Your Answer _____

_____

Q–108

Who wrote *Poor Richard's Almanac*?

Your Answer _____

_____

Correct Answers

A–106

The policy would lure away their labor supply and drive up wages.

A–107

Democrat Republicans

A–108

Benjamin Franklin

Questions

Q–109

Why was the new tariff bill of 1828 known as the "Tariff of Abominations" by Southern planters?

Your Answer _____

_____

Q–110

What was the Pinckney Treaty of 1795?

Your Answer _____

_____

Q–111

How did the 1947 Taft-Hartley Act affect unions?

Your Answer _____

_____

Correct Answers

A–109

The finished bill included higher import duties for many goods that were bought by Southern planters.

A–110

The Pinckney Treaty was a treaty between Spain and the United States whereby Spain opened up the Mississippi River to American trade and recognized the 31st parallel as being the northern boundary of Florida.

A–111

The Taft-Hartley Act made the "closed shop" illegal; ended the practice of employers collecting dues for unions; and forbade such actions as secondary boycotts, jurisdictional strikes, and featherbedding.

Questions

Q–112

What new, potent illegal drug appeared in urban America during the 1980s?

Your Answer _____

Q–113

What was the Non-Intercourse Act? What replaced it when it expired?

Your Answer _____

Q–114

What controversies surrounded the Treaty of Portsmouth in 1905?

Your Answer _____

Correct Answers

A–112

Crack cocaine

A–113

1) The Non-Intercourse Act was a modified embargo act that opened trade to all nations except France and Great Britain.
2) When it expired in 1810, it was replaced with Macon's Bill No. 2, which gave the president the power to prohibit trade with any nation that violated U.S. neutrality.

A–114

The Treaty of Portsmouth officially ended the Russo-Japanese War. Although Japan was the clear winner of the war, the Japanese did not feel that they received fair territorial and financial compensation from Russia. President Theodore Roosevelt was awarded a Nobel Peace Prize for helping to negotiate the treaty.

Questions

Q–115

When did the Communists take over China? Who was the leader of the Communist forces?

Your Answer _____

_____

Q–116

What was the Hawley-Smoot Tariff? When was it passed? Why is it still considered controversial?

Your Answer _____

_____

Q–117

Why did many farmers go into debt during the Civil War?

Your Answer _____

_____

Correct Answers

A–115

1) 1949
2) Mao Tse-tung

A–116

1) The Hawley-Smoot Tariff raised duties on both agricultural and manufacturer imports.
2) June 1930
3) Historians still argue over whether or not it contributed to the spread of the international depression.

A–117

They overexpanded their operations by buying more land and machinery than they could afford.

Questions

Q–118

What was the "square deal" during the Progressive Era?

Your Answer _____

_____

Q–119

What was John C. Calhoun's reaction to the Tariff of 1832? What was President Jackson's response to Calhoun's position?

Your Answer _____

_____

Q–120

What powers did America's first constitution, the Articles of Confederation, grant the federal government? What was not allowed?

Your Answer _____

_____

Correct Answers

A–118

A policy followed by President Theodore Roosevelt to restrain corporate monopoly and promote economic competition

A–119

1) Calhoun resigned from the vice presidency and drew up the Ordinance of Nullification that ordered customs agents to stop collecting duties at Charleston Port.
2) Jackson obtained the Force Bill from Congress authorizing him to use federal troops to enforce the collection of taxes.

A–120

The Articles of Confederation created a weak federal government that allowed the federal government to make war and foreign policy, but it did not allow the national government to levy taxes, raise troops, or regulate trade.

Questions

Q–121

Which amendment guarantees freedom of speech, press, and religion?

Your Answer _____

Q–122

Who wrote *The Feminine Mystique* in 1963? What was the main point of the book?

Your Answer _____

Q–123

Which abolitionist started the newspaper *The Liberator* and gave new life to the abolitionist movement?

Your Answer _____

Correct Answers

A–121

The First Amendment

A–122

1) Betty Friedan
2) That middle-class society stifled women and did not allow them to use their individual talents

A–123

William Lloyd Garrison

Questions

What did the Transcendentalists believe?

Your Answer _____

Who authored "*The Raven*" and other tales of terror and darkness?

Your Answer _____

What ideas are associated with Marcus Garvey?

Your Answer _____

Correct Answers

A–124

Their objective was to transcend the intellect and strive for emotional understanding to attain unity with God.

A–125

Edgar Allan Poe

A–126

Marcus Garvey advocated black racial pride, separatism, and a return of blacks to Africa rather than integration.

Questions

Who were the muckrakers?

Your Answer _____

_____

Who was W. E. B. DuBois?

Your Answer _____

_____

What kind of educational opportunities existed for southern women before the Civil War?

Your Answer _____

_____

Correct Answers

A–127

The muckrackers were investigative journalists and authors who favored progressive political, economic, and social reforms in the early 1900s.

A–128

W. E. B. DuBois was an African American intellectual militant who founded the Niagara Movement and fought for the rights of his race.

A–129

Education for southern women was rare; what little there was centered on the "domestic arts."

Questions

Q–130

What happened at Kent State University in May 1970?

Your Answer _____

Q–131

True or False: The canal system that was built in the first part of the nineteenth century generally ran in a north-south direction.

Your Answer _____

Q–132

Who invented the cotton gin? What was its effect on the South?

Your Answer _____

Correct Answers

A–130

Four antiwar student protesters were killed by the Ohio National Guard. This inflamed students across the country and intensified the protests against the Vietnam War.

A–131

False. The canals ran east-west, linking the old East with the new West.

A–132

1) Eli Whitney created the cotton gin, which created a faster and more efficient means to separate the cotton fibers from the seeds.
2) This machine made the use of slave labor to farm cotton more efficient and thus more profitable.

Questions

Q–133

What three industries developed in the South during the 1880s?

Your Answer _____

_____

Q–134

What led to the Panic of 1873?

Your Answer _____

_____

Q–135

Who founded the Standard Oil Company and helped develop the modern oil industry in the United States?

Your Answer _____

_____

Correct Answers

A–133

Textiles, steel, and tobacco

A–134

The overexpansion of railroads, an economic down-turn in Europe, and the failure of the American financial firm of Jay Cooke

A–135

John D. Rockefeller

Questions

Q–136

How was the Democratic Party split in 1948?

Your Answer _____

_____

Q–137

How did Theodore Roosevelt become president?

Your Answer _____

_____

Q–138

What were "Jim Crow" laws?

Your Answer _____

_____

Correct Answers

A–136

1) Many southern Democrats, angered by President Harry Truman's support of civil rights, split off to form the Dixiecrat Party headed by South Carolina Governor Strom Thurmond.
2) The Progressive Party was formed as a protest against the Cold War policies of the Truman administration. It nominated former Vice President Henry Wallace for president.

A–137

He was vice president when President William McKinley was assassinated.

A–138

They were laws that separated the races in the South for a century after the Civil War.

Questions

Q–139

What was the Compromise of 1877?

Your Answer _____

_____

Q–140

Who were Sacco and Vanzetti?

Your Answer _____

_____

Q–141

How did the Chicago World's Fair of 1893 influence the appearance of cities?

Your Answer _____

_____

Correct Answers

A–139

The Compromise of 1877 was an agreement under which Rutherford B. Hayes promised to show consideration for southern interests, end Reconstruction, and withdraw the remaining federal troops from the South in exchange for the Democrats going along with his election to the presidency.

A–140

Sacco and Vanzetti were Italian immigrants and admitted anarchists convicted of murder in 1920 and sentenced to death. Many believe their convictions were based on the political radicalism of the defendants, not evidence.

A–141

The fair led to the expansion of urban public parks and encouraged the "city beautiful" movement across the country.

Questions

Q–142

Describe the composition of the "New Deal coalition."

Your Answer _____

_____

Q–143

What was the major reason for the improved economy during most of the 1920s?

Your Answer _____

_____

Q–144

Describe five economic effects of the Depression.

Your Answer _____

_____

Correct Answers

A–142

1) Solid South
2) Ethnic groups in big cities
3) Midwestern farmers
4) Union workers
5) Blacks

A–143

Improved industrial efficiency that resulted in lower prices for goods

A–144

1) Unemployment rose to 25 percent.
2) National income dropped 54 percent.
3) Labor income fell about 41 percent.
4) Industrial production dropped about 51 percent.
5) By 1932, 22 percent of the nation's banks had failed.

Questions

Q–145

Who unionized Mexican-American farmworkers?

Your Answer _____

Q–146

What antiunion measure did President Ronald Reagan take in 1981?

Your Answer _____

Q–147

In what ways does the Federal Reserve try to regulate the economy?

Your Answer _____

Correct Answers

A–145

Cesar Chavez

A–146

He fired all striking air-traffic controllers.

A–147

The Federal Reserve will lower interest rates to stimulate the economy and raise interest rates to regulate inflation.

Questions

Q–148

Which inventor built the steamboats the *Clermont* in 1807 and the *New Orleans* in 1811?

Your Answer _____

_____

Q–149

Who was John Paul Jones?

Your Answer _____

_____

Q–150

Which president offered amnesty to Americans who had fled the draft and gone to other countries during the Vietnam War?

Your Answer _____

Correct Answers

A–148

Robert Fulton

A–149

John Paul Jones was the most famous of the American naval leaders who captured British ships and carried out audacious raids along the coast of Britain. He is considered the father of the U.S. Navy.

A–150

President Jimmy Carter

Questions

Q–151

What was the Wagner Act? When was it enacted?

Your Answer _____

_____

Q–152

What were the main products of midwestern family farms in the 1850s?

Your Answer _____

_____

Q–153

Who was Henry Ford?

Your Answer _____

_____

Correct Answers

A–151

1) The Wagner Act reaffirmed labor's right to unionize, prohibited unfair labor practices, and created the National Labor Relations Board (NLRB) to oversee and ensure fairness in labor-management relations.
2) May 1935

A–152

Grain and livestock

A–153

Henry Ford was an automobile manufacturer who introduced the continuous flow process on the automobile assembly line. He became one of the most famous and wealthy industrialists of the 20th century.

Questions

Q–154

What was President Andrew Jackson's policy regarding Indian tribes?

Your Answer _____

Q–155

What policy toward Cuba did Assistant Secretary of the Navy Theodore Roosevelt advocate?

Your Answer _____

Q–156

What was the "Domino Theory"?

Your Answer _____

Correct Answers

A–154

He supported the removal of all eastern Indian tribes west of the Mississippi.

A–155

Direct military intervention by the United States

A–156

The Domino Theory justified American involvement in Vietnam by arguing that if Vietnam fell to the Communists, all of Southeast Asia would eventually fall as well.

Questions

Q–157

What bold diplomatic initiatives did President Nixon begin in 1972?

Your Answer _____

_____

Q–158

What were the three main reasons for the American declaration of war against Spain in 1898?

Your Answer _____

_____

Q–159

What did Shays' Rebellion indicate to many Americans?

Your Answer _____

_____

Correct Answers

A-157

Nixon sent National Security Advisor Henry Kissinger on secret missions to plan summit meetings in both China and the Soviet Union.

A-158

1) Loss of markets
2) Threats to Americans in Cuba
3) The inability of Spain and Cuba to resolve the Cuban revolution

A-159

Shays' Rebellion alerted Americans that a stronger central government was needed to control violent uprisings.

Questions

Q–160

Name the most important provisions of the 1964 Civil Rights Act.

Your Answer _____

_____

Q–161

What three kinds of political reforms took place at the state level during the early 1900s?

Your Answer _____

_____

Q–162

Why did the women's rights movement become stronger during the 1870s and 1880s?

Your Answer _____

_____

Correct Answers

A–160

The 1964 Civil Rights Act outlawed racial discrimination by employers and unions, created the Equal Employment Opportunity Commission to enforce the law, and eliminated the remaining restrictions on black voting.

A–161

Primary elections, initiative and referendum, and the rooting out of political machines

A–162

Because millions of women worked outside the home and were active in social reform movements

Questions

Q–163

What was the Underground Railroad?

Your Answer _____

_____

Q–164

Where and when did the first feminist meeting take place?

Your Answer _____

_____

Q–165

What was the role of women in society immediately after World War II?

Your Answer _____

_____

Correct Answers

A–163

The Underground Railroad was a system by which northern abolitionists smuggled escaped slaves to permanent freedom in Canada.

A–164

Seneca Falls, New York, 1848

A–165

A cult of female domesticity re-emerged. Countless magazine articles promoted the concept that a woman's place was in the home.

Questions

Q–166

Explain the demographic trend called "white flight."

Your Answer _____

Q–167

What were "Hoovervilles"?

Your Answer _____

Q–168

What spurred consumer interest and demand in the 1920s?

Your Answer _____

Correct Answers

A–166

As blacks moved into the northern and midwestern cities, whites moved to the suburbs.

A–167

Makeshift shacks that housed hundreds of thousands of homeless people in empty spaces around cities during the Depression

A–168

A great increase in professional advertising using newspapers, magazines, radio, billboards, and other media

Questions

Q–169

What explains the tremendous growth of the suburbs during the 1920s?

Your Answer

Q–170

What were the two arguments in the Webster-Hayne Debate?

Your Answer

Q–171

What were "The Federalist Papers"?

Your Answer

Correct Answers

A–169

Better transportation through streetcars, commuter railroads, and automobiles, as well as the easy availability of financing for home construction

A–170

Senator Robert Hayne of South Carolina argued against protective tariffs and referred to nullification as a solution. Senator Daniel Webster of Massachusetts argued that the Union was indissoluble and that the federal government was sovereign over the individual states.

A–171

The papers were written as a series of eighty-five newspaper articles by Alexander Hamilton, John Jay, and James Madison. They expounded the virtues of the proposed new Constitution, defining a strong central government for the young United States.

Questions

Q–172

What sports celebrity became a cultural icon during the 1920s and helped make baseball America's sport?

Your Answer _____

_____

Q–173

The _____ movement of the nineteenth century emphasized the emotions and feelings over rationality.

Your Answer _____

_____

Q–174

What issue split the antiwar movement during the 1960s?

Your Answer _____

_____

Correct Answers

A–172

Babe Ruth

A–173

Romantic

A–174

It split between those favoring violence and those opposed to it.

Questions

Q–175

What was the 1963 March on Washington?

Your Answer _____

Q–176

What did the National Association for the Advancement of Colored People (NAACP) advocate?

Your Answer _____

Q–177

Who was eligible to join the Civilian Conservation Corps? What kind of work did the Corps do?

Your Answer _____

Correct Answers

A–175

The 1963 March on Washington was a demonstration by over 200,000 people in support of the 1963 Civil Rights Bill. It was at this demonstration that Martin Luther King, Jr., gave his famous "I Have a Dream" speech.

A–176

An end to racial segregation

A–177

1) Young men ages eighteen to twenty-four from families on relief
2) They worked on flood control, soil conservation, and forest projects under the direction of the War Department.

Questions

Q–178

What was the primary reason for the Race Riots of 1919? What city had the worst riots?

Your Answer _____

_____

Q–179

What farmers' organizations were formed after the Civil War?

Your Answer _____

_____

Q–180

In 1818 the _____ _____, from Wheeling, Virginia, to Cumberland, Maryland, linking the Potomac with the Ohio River, was completed.

Your Answer _____

_____

Correct Answers

A–178

1) White hostility based on competition for lower-paying jobs and black encroachment into white neighborhoods
2) The Chicago riot was the worst, lasting thirteen days and leaving 38 dead, 520 wounded, and 1,000 families homeless.

A–179

The National Grange and the Farmers' Alliances

A–180

National Road

Questions

How did Americans' outrage during the XYZ Affair affect American-French trade relations?

Your Answer _____

_____

What was the Roosevelt Corollary to the Monroe Doctrine?

Your Answer _____

_____

What incident led Austria to interfere in Serbia in 1914?

Your Answer _____

_____

Correct Answers

A–181

After the XYZ Affair, President John Adams suspended trade relations with the French and authorized American ship captains to attack armed French vessels.

A–182

The Roosevelt Corollary established the U.S. policy of intervening in the internal affairs of Latin American nations to keep European nations from using military force to collect debts.

A–183

The assassination of the heir to the Austrian Hapsburg empire

Questions

Q–184

What Supreme Court decision upheld President Franklin Roosevelt's 1942 order that Japanese Americans be relocated to concentration camps? What year was the decision made? When were the camps closed?

Your Answer _____

_____

Q–185

Describe the main provisions of the Social Security Act.

Your Answer _____

_____

Q–186

What three cities each had a population of over 1 million by the year 1900?

Your Answer _____

_____

Correct Answers

A–184

1) *Korematsu v. United States*
2) 1944
3) March 1946

A–185

The Social Security Act established a retirement plan for persons over age sixty-five funded by a tax or wages paid equally by employee and employer. The act also provided matching funds to the states for aid to the blind, handicapped, and dependent children.

A–186

New York, Chicago, and Philadelphia

Questions

Q–187

How did the immigrants from the "old immigration" movement differ from those in the "new immigration" movement?

Your Answer _____

_____

Q–188

What was the purpose of John Brown's raid on Harper's Ferry? What was the reaction to this event?

Your Answer _____

_____

Q–189

What major waterway system linked the Hudson River at Albany, New York, with Lake Erie?

Your Answer _____

_____

Correct Answers

A–187

The earlier immigrants came mostly from northern Europe, while the later immigrants came mostly from southern and eastern Europe.

A–188

1) John Brown hoped to capture the federal arsenal and start a slave uprising.
2) Many in the North began to view Brown as a martyr, but many in the South saw this as evidence that the North wanted to end slavery. This event also played on one of the South's deepest fears, slave revolt.

A–189

The Erie Canal

Questions

What factors explain the drop in labor union membership in the 1980s?

Your Answer _____

_____

What was the Specie Redemption Act of 1875?

Your Answer _____

_____

Which American colonies prospered from England's mercantilistic policy?

Your Answer _____

_____

Correct Answers

A–190

The economy was shifting from heavy industry to electronics and service industries.

A–191

The Specie Redemption Act called for retiring the greenbacks and adopting the gold standard for money by 1879.

A–192

New England—it encouraged trade and large-scale shipbuilding.

Questions

Q–193

What was the objective of the Agricultural Adjustment Act of 1933?

Your Answer _____

_____

Q–194

How did the vote of 700,000 blacks, in the southern states under military rule, affect the 1868 election?

Your Answer _____

_____

Q–195

What was the immediate result of the Compromise of 1850?

Your Answer _____

_____

Correct Answers

A–193

The act sought to return farm prices to parity with those of the 1909 to 1914 period.

A–194

The black vote probably gave the election to Ulysses S. Grant.

A–195

The issue of slavery in the territories seemed to have been permanently settled and sectional harmony returned.

Questions

Q–196

Why is the Jacksonian era known as the "age of the common man"?

Your Answer _____

_____

Q–197

_____ _____, an English political Enlightenment philosopher, advocated the overthrow of government that abuses the subjects' rights of life, liberty, and property.

Your Answer _____

_____

Q–198

Who were the Wobblies?

Your Answer _____

_____

Correct Answers

A–196

Since most states had eliminated the property requirement for voting, the electorate was broadened to include almost all white males over twenty-one years of age.

A–197

John Locke

A–198

The Wobblies were members of a radical labor organization called the Industrial Workers of the World (I.W.W.). In the early 1900s, this organization was successful in the textile industry and the western mining industry.

Questions

Q-199

What happened in the Rosenberg Case?

Your Answer _____

_____

Q-200

What lucrative trade was opened by the French and the Indians?

Your Answer _____

_____

Q-201

What was the effect of the first New Deal policies on unemployment?

Your Answer _____

_____

Correct Answers

A–199

In 1950, Julius and Ethel Rosenberg were charged with giving atomic secrets to the Soviet Union. They were convicted and executed in 1953.

A–200

The fur trade

A–201

Unemployment dropped from about 25 percent of nonfarm workers in 1933 to about 20 percent in 1935, but this unemployment rate was still much higher than the 3.2 percent of pre-Depression 1929.

Questions

Q-202

What made federal intervention in the 1902 coal strike different from previous strikes?

Your Answer _____

_____

Q-203

What was the focus of the Scopes trial?

Your Answer _____

_____

Q-204

How did the United States respond to Iraq's invasion of Kuwait in 1990?

Your Answer _____

_____

Correct Answers

A–202

The 1902 intervention was the first time that the federal government intervened in a labor dispute without automatically siding with management. Teddy Roosevelt was the first president to deal with both labor and management on equal terms.

A–203

The focus of the Scopes trial was whether evolution should be taught in the public schools. Although the defendant, a high school biology teacher named John Thomas Scopes, was convicted of violating a Tennessee law that forbade the teaching of evolution, the trial was largely seen as a victory for free speech.

A–204

The United States first sent 100,000 troops to Saudi Arabia as part of Operation Desert Shield. The United States then increased troop levels to 400,000 and set a January 15, 1991, deadline for Iraqi withdrawal from Kuwait. Operation Desert Storm (the First Gulf War) began on January 17, 1991.

Questions

Q–205

What was the Kellogg-Briand Pact? What was its major flaw?

Your Answer _____

_____

Q–206

Why did American troops invade Mexico in 1914?

Your Answer _____

_____

Q–207

What was the political aftermath of the Mexican War within the United States?

Your Answer _____

_____

Correct Answers

A–205

1) The Kellogg-Briand Pact was a treaty signed at Paris in August 1928 that renounced war as an instrument of national policy.
2) The treaty had no enforcement provisions.

A–206

General Victoriano Huerto rejected President Woodrow Wilson's call for democratic elections in Mexico and the establishment of a constitutional government.

A–207

The Mexican War brought to the surface the issue of slavery in the new territories.

Questions

Q-208

What was the Embargo Act of 1807? How did it affect America?

Your Answer _____

Q-209

Why did the French help the Americans in its struggle against Britain?

Your Answer _____

Q-210

What was "détente" in the 1970's?

Your Answer _____

Correct Answers

A–208

1) The Embargo Act of 1807 prohibited American ships from leaving port for any foreign destination.
2) It resulted in economic depression, especially for the heavily commercial Northeast.

A–209

The French hated Britain after their loss in the Seven Years War and saw the war as a way to weaken Britain by depriving it of its colonies.

A–210

A policy initiated during the Nixon administration that aimed to reduce the amount of tension between the United States and the Soviet Union

Questions

Q–211

What was the Bay of Pigs operation?

Your Answer _____

Q–212

Which Shawnee Indian chief united the Mississippi Valley tribes to reestablish dominance in the old Northwest?

Your Answer _____

Q–213

What were the Intolerable Acts?

Your Answer _____

Correct Answers

A–211

Under President Eisenhower, the CIA trained some 2,000 men for an invasion of Cuba to overthrow Fidel Castro. On April 19, 1961, during John F. Kennedy's administration, this force invaded Cuba at the Bay of Pigs but was routed and forced to surrender.

A–212

Tecumseh

A–213

Americans lumped the Quebec Act with the Coercive Acts and referred to them as the Intolerable Acts.

Questions

What was the Nuclear Test Ban Treaty?

Your Answer _____

What were the revenue-producing crops produced by the southern plantation system—cotton, tobacco, and so on—collectively known as?

Your Answer _____

Which river served as the French gateway to the interior of North America?

Your Answer _____

Correct Answers

A–214

The Nuclear Test Ban Treaty, which was signed in 1963 by all major powers except France and China, banned the atmospheric testing of nuclear weapons.

A–215

Cash crops

A–216

The St. Lawrence River

Questions

What banking reform came out of the Panic of 1907?

Your Answer _____

What was the Gilded Age?

Your Answer _____

Which new industry was the largest consumer of iron in the nineteenth century?

Your Answer _____

Correct Answers

A–217

Establishment of the Federal Reserve System

A–218

The period between the 1870s and 1890s in America

A–219

The railroad industry

Questions

Q-220

Who was Dorothea Dix?

Your Answer _____

Q-221

Who escaped from his owner and established his own newspaper, the *North Star*?

Your Answer _____

Q-222

What did the Sixteenth Amendment to the Constitution establish?

Your Answer _____

Correct Answers

A–220

Dorothea Dix was a reformer who advocated for more humane treatment for the mentally incompetent in mental asylums.

A–221

Frederick Douglass

A–222

The amendment provided for a graduated income tax.

Questions

Q–223

What was the tactic known as "waving the bloody shirt" after the Civil War?

Your Answer _____

_____

Q–224

What prompted President Franklin Roosevelt to issue an executive order establishing the Fair Employment Practice Committee in June of 1941? What was the purpose of the committee?

Your Answer _____

_____

Q–225

What did the Federal Trade Commission Act of 1914 do?

Your Answer _____

_____

Correct Answers

A–223

It was a tactic in which Republicans urged northerners to vote for them in support of the men who died during the Civil War. It suggested that a Democratic victory would be the same as a Confederate victory.

A–224

1) Black union leader A. Philip Randolph threatened to lead a black march on Washington to demand equal access to defense jobs.
2) The purpose of the committee was to ensure consideration for minorities in defense employment.

A–225

The law prohibited all unfair trade practices without defining them, and created a commission of five members appointed by the president. The commission was empowered to issue cease and desist orders to corporations, stop actions considered to be in restraint of trade, and bring lawsuits if the orders were not obeyed.

Questions

Q-226

How did President Lincoln respond to the Confederate firing on Fort Sumter?

Your Answer _____

_____

Q-227

The _____ _____ required colonists to pay for the maintenance of British troops stationed in their area.

Your Answer _____

_____

Q-228

What encouraged freer sexual practices during the 1960s?

Your Answer _____

_____

Correct Answers

A–226

Lincoln declared the existence of an insurrection and called for 75,000 volunteers to put it down.

A–227

Quartering Act

A–228

New methods of birth control, particularly the birth control pill

Questions

What is NAFTA? Who were its most prominent critics?

Your Answer _____

_____

How did World War I affect the Prohibition movement?

Your Answer _____

_____

What were the Sack of Lawrence and the Pottawatomie Massacre?

Your Answer _____

_____

Correct Answers

A–229

1) The North American Free Trade Agreement eliminated most tariffs and other trade barriers between the United States, Canada, and Mexico.
2) Organized labor and Ross Perot

A–230

Proponents of Prohibition stressed the need for military personnel to be sober and the need to conserve grain for food.

A–231

Both occurred during the guerrilla war in "Bleeding Kansas" in the 1850's. At the Sack of Lawrence, pro-slavery forces attacked free-soilers. In response, John Brown led antislavery forces in slaughtering several pro-slavery supporters at the Pottawatomie Massacre.

Questions

Why may it be said that the Enlightenment further weakened the church's influence in society?

Your Answer _____

What did the GI Bill of 1944 do?

Your Answer _____

Who was the first woman appointed to a cabinet position?

Your Answer _____

Correct Answers

A–232

The Enlightenment placed less faith in God as an active force in the universe.

A–233

The GI Bill provided returning servicemen after World War II with $13 billion in aid ranging from education to housing.

A–234

Frances Perkins was appointed Secretary of Labor by President Franklin Roosevelt in 1933.

Questions

Q–235

What was President Theodore Roosevelt's attitude toward trusts?

Your Answer _____

_____

Q–236

What three groups formed the Republican Party? What was their unifying principle?

Your Answer _____

_____

Q–237

What was a common criticism of universities by student protesters during the 1960s?

Your Answer _____

_____

Correct Answers

A–235

He believed that illegal monopolies should be broken up and that the federal government should regulate large corporations for the good of the public.

A–236

1) Northern Democrats, former Whigs, and Know-Nothings
2) All three groups believed slavery should be banned from the territories.

A–237

The common criticism was that bureaucracies were indifferent to students' needs.

Questions

Q–238

What was the Bonus Army, why was it forced to leave Washington, and who commanded the force that removed its members?

Your Answer _____

_____

Q–239

What did Gabriel Prosser, Denmark Vesey, and Nat Turner all have in common?

Your Answer _____

_____

Q–240

What farm policies did the Greenback-Labor Party advocate?

Your Answer _____

_____

Correct Answers

A–238

1) The Bonus Army was a group of about 14,000 unemployed veterans who went to Washington in the summer of 1932 to lobby Congress for immediate payment of the bonus that had been approved in 1924 for payment in 1945.
2) After two veterans were killed in a clash with the police, President Herbert Hoover, calling them insurrectionists and communists, ordered the army to remove them.
3) General Douglas MacArthur

A–239

They all plotted or led uprisings of black slaves against their white masters in the early 1800's.

A–240

1) Inflated farm prices
2) The cooperative marketing of produce

Questions

What percent of the workforce was unemployed as a result of the Depression of 1893?

Your Answer _____

_____

How did the Glorious Revolution of 1658 affect the English monarchy?

Your Answer _____

_____

Which Ottowa chief led a bloody Indian uprising, vowing to drown the entire white population in the sea?

Your Answer _____

_____

Correct Answers

A–241

20 percent

A–242

The Glorious Revolution of 1658 replaced Catholic James with his Protestant daughter Mary and her husband William of Orange as England's monarchs.

A–243

Pontiac

Questions

Q-244

How did Americans initially respond to the Coercive Acts?

Your Answer _____

_____

Q-245

What were the provisions of the Treaty of Paris that ended the American Revolution?

Your Answer _____

_____

Q-246

What did the Nineteenth Amendment provide for and when did Congress approve it?

Your Answer _____

_____

Correct Answers

A–244

They called the First Continental Congress in September 1774.

A–245

America's western boundary became the Mississippi River, and Great Britain agreed to remove all of its western outposts.

A–246

The Nineteenth Amendment provided for woman suffrage, and Congress approved it in 1919.

Questions

Q–247

What four policies did the Fourteenth Amendment establish?

Your Answer _____

_____

Q–248

What two main factions existed at the Second Continental Congress?

Your Answer _____

_____

Q–249

Describe the origins of the Free Speech Movement on American college campuses in the mid 1960's.

Your Answer _____

_____

Correct Answers

A–247

1) The Fourteenth Amendment forbade states to deny various rights to citizens.
2) It forbade the paying of the Confederate debt.
3) It denied Congressional representation to states that did not give blacks the right to vote.
4) It made former Confederates ineligible to hold public office.

A–248

1) New Englanders who leaned toward declaring independence from Britain
2) A group, led by John Dickinson of Pennsylvania, which drew its strength from the middle colonies and was not yet ready to declare its independence

A–249

Students at the University of California, Berkeley, staged sit-ins in 1964 to protest the prohibition of political canvassing on campus. Led by Mario Savio, the movement changed from emphasizing student rights to criticizing the bureaucracy of American society.

Questions

Q-250

The eighteenth-century European intellectual movement is known as the _____.

Your Answer _____

Q-251

What was the purpose of the early antislavery movement?

Your Answer _____

Q-252

What was the White Citizens' Council?

Your Answer _____

Correct Answers

A–250

Enlightenment

A–251

The movement advocated the purchase and colonization of slaves.

A–252

The White Citizens' Council was the leading organization throughout the South in resisting the *Brown v. Board of Education* decision in 1954.

Questions

What organization's membership growth in the 1920s was a reaction against the changing and modernizing American society?

Your Answer _____

_____

Which two groups of immigrant workers were discriminated against and fought for economic survival in California during the 1870s?

Your Answer _____

_____

What did immigrants obtain in exchange for giving political support to city governments?

Your Answer _____

_____

Correct Answers

A–253

Ku Klux Klan

A–254

The Irish and the Chinese

A–255

Jobs, housing, and social services

Questions

Q–256

What encouraged 6,000 Americans to travel westward over the Oregon Trail during the first half of the 1840s?

Your Answer _____

_____

Q–257

What was the Great Awakening?

Your Answer _____

_____

Q–258

What two national labor organizations were formed during the 1860s?

Your Answer _____

_____

Correct Answers

A–256

Reports by fur traders and missionaries about Oregon's favorable soil and climate

A–257

The Great Awakening was a series of religious revivals throughout the colonies between 1720 and 1740.

A–258

The National Labor Union and the Knights of Labor

Questions

Q–259

What two labor-saving machines were midwestern farmers using by 1860?

Your Answer

Q–260

In 1994, how did the Federal Reserve respond to the fears of increased inflation?

Your Answer

Q–261

List three main manufacturing industries in the South during the 1820s and 1830s.

Your Answer

Correct Answers

A–259

Cyrus McCormick's mechanical reaper and the mechanical thresher

A–260

By beginning a series of interest rate increases

A–261

1) Textiles
2) Iron production
3) Flour milling

Questions

Q–262

What were the positions of the "Moral Majority" political movement?

Your Answer _____

Q–263

What memorable slogan did President Franklin Roosevelt use in his inaugural speech on March 4, 1933?

Your Answer _____

Q–264

Name the most famous scandal of the Harding administration.

Your Answer _____

Correct Answers

A–262

Members of the Moral Majority favored prayer in school, opposed abortion and the Equal Rights Amendment, and supported a strong national defense.

A–263

"The only thing we have to fear is fear itself."

A–264

The most famous scandal of the Harding administration was the Teapot Dome Scandal. Secretary of the Interior Albert B. Fall was convicted, fined, and imprisoned for accepting bribes in exchange for leasing oil reserves at Teapot Dome, Wyoming.

Questions

Q–265

John Quincy Adams's supporters called themselves
_____ _____.

Your Answer _____

Q–266

What is the Bill of Rights?

Your Answer _____

Q–267

Who were the "Freedom Riders"?

Your Answer _____

Correct Answers

A–265

National Republicans

A–266

The Bill of Rights is the first ten amendments to the Constitution, which embody guarantees of personal liberties for Americans.

A–267

The Freedom Riders were a group of blacks and whites who traveled across the South in 1961 to test federal enforcement of regulations prohibiting discrimination.

Questions

Q–268

Who became president of the Tuskegee Institute in 1881?

Your Answer _____

Q–269

How did industrial innovation benefit farming during the 19th century?

Your Answer _____

Q–270

Why did Great Britain want the Puget Sound area north of the Columbia River in the Oregon Territory?

Your Answer _____

Correct Answers

A–268

Booker T. Washington

A–269

Many of industry's technological developments and inventions were applied to farm machinery, which in turn enabled farmers to produce more food more cheaply.

A–270

Because Puget Sound is one of only three natural harbors on the Pacific Coast

Questions

Q–271

Why did Spain urge the pope to draw up a "Line of Demarcation" in the New World?

Your Answer _____

_____

Q–272

Which country was England's chief maritime rival during the seventeenth century?

Your Answer _____

_____

Q–273

How did colonial merchants achieve the repeal of the Stamp Act?

Your Answer _____

_____

Correct Answers

A–271

The Line of Demarcation favored Spain over Portugal, as Spain was entitled to all lands west of Cape Verdes Island. Portugal, however, had a stronger navy.

A–272

Holland

A–273

They boycotted British goods.

Questions

Q–274

Why did Congress resort to printing large quantities of paper money under the Articles of Confederation?

Your Answer _____

_____

Q–275

What did the Emancipation Proclamation do?

Your Answer _____

_____

Q–276

What was the purpose of the War Industries Board?

Your Answer _____

_____

Correct Answers

A–274

Congress needed money to finance the war but was unable to tax its citizens.

A–275

The Emancipation Proclamation freed all slaves in areas still in rebellion against the United States.

A–276

The War Industries Board coordinated industrial mobilization by allocating raw materials, standardizing manufactured products, and instituting strict production and purchasing controls.

Questions

Q-277

How did the United States respond to Japan gaining military control of southern Indochina from Vichy France in 1940?

Your Answer _____

_____

Q-278

What was the purpose of the Reconstruction Finance Corporation (RFC)?

Your Answer _____

_____

Q-279

What economic and foreign policies did President James Polk change during his presidency?

Your Answer _____

_____

Correct Answers

A–277

The United States responded by freezing Japanese funds in the United States, closing the Panama Canal to Japan, activating the Philippine Militia, and placing an embargo on the export of oil and other vital products to Japan.

A–278

Chartered by Congress in 1932, the RFC made loans to railroads, banks, and other financial institutions. Its aim was to prevent the failure of basic firms on which many other elements of the economy depended.

A–279

1) Economic policies: Established a national treasury system, lowered tariffs
2) Foreign policies: Settled Oregon boundary dispute, acquired the Southwest and California

Questions

Q–280

List two reasons why the West was most severely hit by the Depression of 1819.

Your Answer _____

Q–281

What was the "Oregon Fever" of the 1840s?

Your Answer _____

Q–282

What were the three main goals of the "new imperialism" of the 1870s?

Your Answer _____

Correct Answers

A–280

1) Economic dependency
2) Heavy speculation in western lands

A–281

Thousands of settlers trekked across the Great Plains and the Rocky Mountains to settle in the fertile Willamette valley in Oregon.

A–282

1) Markets for surplus industrial production
2) Access to needed raw materials
3) Opportunities for overseas investment during a time of domestic economic depression

Questions

Q–283

What factors contributed to the economic slump of the early 1970s?

Your Answer _____

_____

Q–284

What abuses did many railroads practice during the 1870s and 1880s?

Your Answer _____

_____

Q–285

Why was the Federal Housing Administration (FHA) created?

Your Answer _____

_____

Correct Answers

A–283

1) Federal deficits
2) International competition
3) Rising energy costs

A–284

They fixed prices, demanded kickbacks, and set discriminatory freight rates.

A–285

The FHA was created to insure long-term, low-interest mortgages for home construction and repair.

Questions

What were the terms of the Pure Food and Drug Act of 1906?

Your Answer _____

_____

Q–287

What were the main provisions of the Fugitive Slave Act of 1850? What was the northern response to it?

Your Answer _____

_____

Q–288

What prompted President Franklin Roosevelt's ill-fated "court packing" proposal?

Your Answer _____

_____

Correct Answers

A–286

The act prohibited the manufacture, sale, and transportation of foods and drugs that were adulterated or fraudulently labeled.

A–287

1) Alleged slaves in the North were denied a trial by jury, and U.S. citizens were required to help capture and return alleged fugitive slaves.
2) Several riots broke out in the North, and some states passed personal liberty laws in opposition.

A–288

Several of his New Deal programs had been struck down by the Supreme Court and he wanted to balance out the power of older, conservative judges on the Court.

Questions

Q–289

What policies regarding railroads and money did farm groups advocate during the 1870s and 1880s?

Your Answer _____

_____

Q–290

What did the Sherman Silver Purchase Act of 1890 provide? What were its results?

Your Answer _____

_____

Q–291

What explains the rising U.S. trade deficits of the 1980s?

Your Answer _____

_____

Correct Answers

A–289

They wanted government regulation of railroads, currency inflation, and the use of both gold and silver.

A–290

1) The Sherman Silver Purchase Act called for the purchase of 4.5 million ounces of silver each month at market prices and for the backing of Treasury notes by both gold and silver.
2) It led to inflation and lower gold reserves.

A–291

U.S. management and engineering skills had fallen behind Japan and Germany, and the United States provided an open market to foreign businesses.

Questions

Q–292

What three epidemics were prevalent in urban areas of the 1830s and 1840s?

Your Answer _____

_____

Q–293

Who invented the sewing machine?

Your Answer _____

_____

Q–294

What were the terms of the Gadsden Purchase? What was its purpose?

Your Answer _____

_____

Correct Answers

A–292

1) Typhoid fever
2) Typhus
3) Cholera

A–293

Elias Howe

A–294

1) The United States bought from Mexico a strip of land along the Gila River in what is now southern New Mexico and Arizona.
2) Its purpose was to provide a good route for a transcontinental railroad across the southern part of the United States.

Questions

Where was an isthmian canal proposed? Where did the United States build the canal? When did the canal open?

Your Answer _____

_____

Where was the first atomic bomb exploded? When was it exploded?

Your Answer _____

_____

What was the Open Door Policy?

Your Answer _____

_____

Correct Answers

A–295

1) Nicaragua and Panama
2) Panama
3) 1914

A–296

1) Alamogordo, New Mexico
2) July 16, 1945

A–297

The Open Door Policy was an American policy designed to protect China's political independence and promote equal opportunity of trade with that country.

Questions

Q-298

Who was the only Democrat elected president in the half century after the Civil War?

Your Answer _____

_____

Q-299

Why did the southern population move to the newly opened Gulf States?

Your Answer _____

_____

Q-300

What did Thomas Edison invent?

Your Answer _____

_____

Correct Answers

A–298

Grover Cleveland

A–299

They could grow cotton and sugar cane in these areas.

A–300

Edison invented electrical devices, including the incandescent lamp, the mimeograph, and the phonograph.

Questions

Q–301

What main principle did the pamphlet titled *Letters from a Farmer in Pennsylvania* point out?

Your Answer _____

_____

Q–302

What was the Submarine Crisis of 1915?

Your Answer _____

_____

Q–303

What was the American response when World War I broke out in Europe in 1914?

Your Answer _____

_____

Correct Answers

A–301

Letters from a Farmer in Pennsylvania was written in the 1770's and pointed out that the Townshend Act violated the principle of no taxation without representation.

A–302

The Germans sank the British liner *Lusitania* off the coast of Ireland on May 7, 1915, resulting in the loss of 1,198 lives, including 128 Americans. President Wilson had argued that Americans had a right as neutrals to travel safely on such ships, and he strongly protested the German action.

A–303

President Wilson issued a proclamation of American neutrality on August 4, 1914.

Questions

Q–304

What was the Lowell System?

Your Answer

Q–305

What was President Franklin D. Roosevelt's inner circle of unofficial advisors called?

Your Answer

Q–306

What did the South threaten to do if the Republicans won the 1856 presidential election?

Your Answer

Correct Answers

A–304

The Lowell System (first developed in Lowell, Massachusetts) was a popular way to staff New England factories. Young farm women were recruited to work in the factories in mill towns and were provided dormitory housing as part of their employment. They worked for short periods of time before getting married.

A–305

The Brain Trust

A–306

Southerners threatened to secede from the United States.

Questions

Q–307

What power was granted to the president that allowed him to check Congress?

Your Answer _____

_____

Q–308

Who were the *peninsulares*?

Your Answer _____

_____

Q–309

True or False: The first Africans brought to Virginia were treated as indentured servants.

Your Answer _____

_____

Correct Answers

A–307

The power to veto Congress's legislation

A–308

The *peninsulares* were natives of Spain who were ranked at the top of New Spain's rigidly stratified society.

A–309

True

Questions

Q–310

Why did the Carolinas attract few settlers in the early colonial period?

Your Answer _____

_____

Q–311

Why did men outnumber women in the Chesapeake Bay colonies?

Your Answer _____

_____

Q–312

In contrast to the Puritans, _____ in Pennsylvania believed that all persons had an "inner light," which allowed them to communicate with God.

Your Answer _____

_____

Correct Answers

A–310

The proprietors set up a hierarchal, almost feudal, society that proved to be totally unworkable.

A–311

Most Chesapeake settlers came to the colonies as indentured servants to work in the tobacco fields.

A–312

Quakers

Questions

Q–313

Why did the Scots-Irish immigrate to the New World? Where did they settle?

Your Answer _____

_____

Q–314

True or False: After 1830, a strong anti-Catholic element was strengthened after waves of immigrants came to America from Catholic Ireland and southern Germany.

Your Answer _____

_____

Q–315

Where did most of the people who settled in Kansas during the 1850s come from? What was their attitude toward slavery?

Your Answer _____

_____

Correct Answers

A–313

1) The Scots-Irish left their homelands due to high rent and economic depression.
2) They settled in the Virginia and North Carolina mountain valleys, beyond the Appalachians.

A–314

True

A–315

1) They were Midwesterners in search of good farmland.
2) They were generally opposed to the spread of slavery.

Questions

Q–316

Which class had economic power and dominated the political and social life of the South?

Your Answer

Q–317

What were the three main purposes of settlement houses?

Your Answer

Q–318

What kind of literature and art gradually replaced Romanticism during the 1880s?

Your Answer

Correct Answers

A–316

The planter class

A–317

The three main purposes were to settle poor immigrants, lobby against sweatshop labor conditions, and call for bans against child labor.

A–318

Realism

Questions

Q–319

What was the relationship between the Depression of 1893 and the formation of the Anti-Saloon League?

Your Answer _____

Q–320

What did the Rural Electrification Administration (REA) do?

Your Answer _____

Q–321

What were Black Codes?

Your Answer _____

Correct Answers

A–319

High unemployment caused by the depression led to increased drunkenness by male workers, which in turn led women to support an anti-saloon movement.

A–320

The REA provided loans and WPA labor to electric cooperatives to build lines into rural areas not served by private companies.

A–321

Restrictions on the freedom of former slaves that were passed by southern states after the end of the Civil War

Questions

Why did California seek admission to the Union as a free state rather than a slave state?

Your Answer _____

_____

True or False: Many colleges were founded as a result of the Great Awakening.

Your Answer _____

_____

What was the Proclamation of 1763? Why was it issued?

Your Answer _____

_____

Correct Answers

A–322

Few slaveholders had come to California because its lawless atmosphere threatened their investment in slaves.

A–323

True. These colleges were established primarily as seminaries for the purpose of training New Light ministers.

A–324

1) The Proclamation of 1763 forbade whites to settle west of the Appalachians.
2) It was issued to improve Anglo-Indian relations, prevent further Indian uprisings, and keep settlers closer to the coast, where they would be more easily controlled.

Questions

Q–325

What did President Abraham Lincoln say about secession in his inaugural address in 1861?

Your Answer _____

_____

Q–326

What territory did Britain gain in the Treaty of Paris (1763)?

Your Answer _____

_____

Q–327

What was the Declaration of Independence?

Your Answer _____

_____

Correct Answers

A–325

Lincoln urged southerners to reconsider and said that states had no right to secede. He said he had no intention of abolishing slavery where it already existed. He announced that the federal government would continue to hold forts and military installations in the South.

A–326

All of Canada and all of the United States east of the Mississippi

A–327

Written largely by Thomas Jefferson and adopted on July 4, 1776, the Declaration of Independence explained to Parliament, loyalists, and the rest of the world why America was justified to separate from Great Britain.

Questions

Q–328

What countries constituted the Triple Entente and Triple Alliance in 1912?

Your Answer _____

_____

Q–329

What was the primary role of African Americans in the army during World War I?

Your Answer _____

_____

Q–330

What were the main tenets of the Three-Fifths Compromise?

Your Answer _____

_____

Correct Answers

A–328

The Triple Entente included Great Britain, France, and Russia. The Triple Alliance included Germany, Austria-Hungary, and Italy (although Italy did not join the Central Powers).

A–329

African Americans were kept in segregated units, usually with white officers, and were used as labor battalions or for other support activities. Some African American units, however, did see combat.

A–330

1) Each slave would count as three-fifths of a person for purposes of taxation and representation.
2) The federal government was prohibited from stopping the importation of slaves prior to 1808.

Questions

Q–331

What did the Civil Rights Act of 1957 establish?

Your Answer _____

_____

Q–332

True or False: Before 1815, schools were primarily sponsored by private institutions.

Your Answer _____

_____

Q–333

Who were the "Mugwumps"? How did they affect the election of 1884?

Your Answer _____

_____

Correct Answers

A–331

The Civil Rights Act of 1957 established a permanent Civil Rights Commission and a Civil Rights Division of the Justice Department that was empowered to prevent interference with the right to vote.

A–332

True

A–333

1) The "Mugwumps" were independent Republicans who favored more civil service reform.
2) They deserted the Republican candidate. This led to the election of Democrat Grover Cleveland.

Questions

Q–334

Why were southerners so wedded to the plantation system?

Your Answer _____

_____

Q–335

Who was Eugene Debs?

Your Answer _____

_____

Q–336

What was the Lancastrian System?

Your Answer _____

_____

Correct Answers

A–334

Cotton was profitable, and planters had most of their money invested in land and slaves. Planters did not have the capital to invest in manufacturing or commerce.

A–335

Leader of the American Railway Union

A–336

The Lancastrian System was an educational system in which older students tutored younger ones. The New York Free School experimented with this method for a time.

Questions

Q–337

What happened to the USS *Maine* in February 1898?

Your Answer _____

Q–338

What was the fastest-growing consumer product in the 1950s?

Your Answer _____

Q–339

True or False: A sizeable number of black slaves worked in towns serving as factory hands, domestics, artisans, and construction workers.

Your Answer _____

Correct Answers

A–337

The USS *Maine* blew up in Havana Harbor; 250 Americans were killed. Although most Americans at the time blamed Spain, most historians believe it was an accidental explosion in a gunpowder magazine.

A–338

Television

A–339

True

Questions

Q–340

Which section of the country had the fewest number of public schools in the 1830s?

Your Answer _____

Q–341

In the first century of American history, women were generally taught _____ skills to prepare them for domestic life.

Your Answer _____

Q–342

True or False: Chief Justice Marshall ruled that only Congress had the right to regulate commerce among states in *Gibbons v. Ogden* in 1824.

Your Answer _____

Correct Answers

A–340

The South

A–341

homemaking

A–342

True

Questions

Q–343

Who became the new Soviet premier in March 1985? What were the characteristics of the new regime?

Your Answer _____

_____

Q–344

What was the Atlantic Charter?

Your Answer _____

_____

Q–345

What happened to the Native American tribes after their defeat by U.S. military forces in the 1870s?

Your Answer _____

_____

Correct Answers

A–343

1) Mikhail Gorbachev
2) A more flexible approach toward both domestic and foreign affairs

A–344

The Atlantic Charter was a statement of principles issued by President Franklin Roosevelt and British Prime Minister Winston Churchill in 1941 that described a postwar world based on self-determination for all nations. It also endorsed the principles of freedom of speech and religion and freedom from want and fear.

A–345

The Native Americans were forced to live on isolated reservations.

Questions

What happened to U.S.-British relations as a result of the Webster-Ashburton Treaty of 1842?

Your Answer _____

_____

What were some of the characteristics of the "Jazz Age" of the 1920s?

Your Answer _____

_____

How did the Public Works Administration work? What was its objective?

Your Answer _____

_____

Correct Answers

A–346

Relations improved as a spirit of compromise and forbearance developed between the two nations.

A–347

Greater sexual promiscuity, drinking, and new forms of dancing considered erotic by the older generation

A–348

1) Federal money was distributed to state and local governments for building projects such as schools, highways, and hospitals.
2) The objective was to "prime the pump" of the economy by creating construction jobs.

Questions

Q-349

Which conquistador conquered the Aztec Empire?

Your Answer _____

Q-350

In which modern-day Canadian city did Samuel de Champlain establish a trading post?

Your Answer _____

Q-351

How did the British authorities react to the Americans' Continental Congress?

Your Answer _____

Correct Answers

A–349

Hernando Cortes

A–350

Quebec

A–351

The British authorities paid little attention to the Americans' grievances and sent more troops to Massachusetts, which they determined to be in a state of rebellion.

Questions

Q–352

How did the U.S. government deal with Tecumseh and his Indian confederacy?

Your Answer _____

_____

Q–353

Why was President James K. Polk reluctant to fight Great Britain over Oregon?

Your Answer _____

_____

Q–354

How did President Lincoln prevent Maryland from seceding?

Your Answer _____

_____

Correct Answers

A–352

William Henry Harrison destroyed Tecumseh's village on Tippecanoe Creek and demolished Tecumseh's dream of an Indian confederacy.

A–353

Polk was more interested in Texas, where trouble was brewing. Also, he considered Oregon unsuitable for agriculture and unavailable for slavery.

A–354

Lincoln suspended the writ of habeas corpus and declared martial law.

Questions

Q–355

What did the 1940 embargo against Japan involve?

Your Answer _____

_____

Q–356

What did the Soviets agree to at the 1945 Yalta Conference?

Your Answer _____

_____

Q–357

How did the Oregon Treaty of 1846 settle the dispute between the United States and Great Britain?

Your Answer _____

_____

Correct Answers

A–355

The embargo involved the export of aviator gasoline, lubricants, and scrap iron. In December 1940, the embargo was extended to include iron ore and pig iron, some chemicals, and machine tools.

A–356

The Soviets agreed to enter the Pacific War within three months after Germany surrendered and agreed to the "Declaration of Liberated Europe," which called for free elections.

A–357

The Oregon Treaty split the disputed Oregon Territory by extending the existing U.S.-Canada boundary of the 49th parallel westward to the Pacific.

Questions

Q–358

The sale of what type of products was responsible for the prosperity of the 1920s?

Your Answer _____

_____

Q–359

What was the economic effect of monopolies, and how did smaller businesses, farmers, and workers respond to monopolies?

Your Answer _____

_____

Q–360

When did President Nixon resign? Who succeeded him?

Your Answer _____

_____

Correct Answers

A–358

Consumer products, such as automobiles, refrigerators, and furniture

A–359

Monopolies lessen competition, and so smaller businesses, farmers, and workers wanted government regulation of industries.

A–360

1) August 8, 1974
2) Vice President Gerald Ford

Questions

Q-361

What did the Selective Service and Training Act do?

Your Answer _____

_____

Q-362

What did the Fifteenth Amendment say?

Your Answer _____

_____

Q-363

What resolutions were drafted by the New England delegates at the Hartford Convention in December 1814?

Your Answer _____

_____

Correct Answers

A–361

Approved in September of 1940, the act created the nation's first peacetime draft.

A–362

The Fifteenth Amendment gave blacks the right to vote.

A–363

They drafted a set of resolutions suggesting nullification and even secession if their interests were not protected against the growing influence of the South and the West.

Questions

Q–364

What is a broad interpretation of the Constitution?

Your Answer _____

_____

Q–365

Where did the Transcendentalist movement originate?

Your Answer _____

_____

Q–366

Why did President John F. Kennedy send the National Guard into Mississippi in the fall of 1962?

Your Answer _____

_____

Correct Answers

A–364

Advocates of a strong central government claimed that the government was given "implied powers" or all powers not expressly denied to it.

A–365

Concord, Massachusetts

A–366

To ensure that a black student, James Meredith, could enroll at the University of Mississippi

Questions

Q–367

Which explorer led three expeditions to the St. Lawrence River, in search of the Northwest Passage?

Your Answer _____

Q–368

What invention by Samuel Morse was first used in 1840 to transmit business news and information?

Your Answer _____

Q–369

What scientist is credited with producing the first atomic chain reaction?

Your Answer _____

Correct Answers

A–367

Jacques Cartier

A–368

The electric telegraph

A–369

Enrico Fermi of the University of Chicago

Questions

Q–370

Which southern state was the first to secede from the Union?

Your Answer _____

Q–371

How did northerners and southerners show opposition to the draft during the Civil War?

Your Answer _____

Q–372

What treaty did Germany defy when it occupied the Rhineland in 1936?

Your Answer _____

Correct Answers

A–370

South Carolina

A–371

New Yorkers rioted while many southerners who were unable to hire a substitute avoided the draft or deserted the army after being drafted.

A–372

The Versailles Treaty

Questions

How did the United States respond to the German invasion of the Soviet Union?

Your Answer _____

_____

What prompted the division in the labor movement between the American Federation of Labor (AFL) and the Congress of Industrial Organizations (CIO)?

Your Answer _____

_____

Why did farm expenses rise during the 1920s?

Your Answer _____

_____

Correct Answers

A–373

The United States extended Lend-Lease assistance to the Soviet Union.

A–374

The CIO wanted to unionize the mass production industries, such as automobiles and rubber, with industrial unions while the AFL continued to try to organize workers in those industries by crafts.

A–375

Farm expenses rose with the cost of more sophisticated machinery and a greater use of chemical fertilizers.

Questions

Q–376

What did the McKinley Tariff of 1890 provide?

Your Answer _____

Q–377

When the Civil War broke out in 1861, what percent of the factories lay in the North?

Your Answer _____

Q–378

True or False: According to the terms of the Treaty of Ghent, the United States was awarded all wartime conquests.

Your Answer _____

Correct Answers

A–376

The McKinley Tariff extended the protective tariff to agricultural and industrial goods and also provided for reciprocal trade agreements.

A–377

81 percent

A–378

False. Both Britain and the United States returned their wartime conquests to each other, thus reestablishing the status quo that was in effect prior to the war.

Questions

Q–379

What excuse did the British use for not evacuating the northwest outposts after the American Revolution?

Your Answer _____

_____

Q–380

When was AIDS discovered? Who were its primary victims?

Your Answer _____

_____

Q–381

What was the aim of the National Industrial Recovery Act of 1934?

Your Answer _____

_____

Correct Answers

A–379

The British refused to leave because the states would not comply with the Treaty of Paris's provision regarding debts and loyalist property.

A–380

1) 1981
2) Homosexual males, hemophiliacs and intravenous drug users

A–381

The National Industrial Recovery Act of 1934 sought to stabilize the economy by preventing extreme competition, labor-management conflicts, and overproduction.

Questions

Q–382

Who founded the American Federation of Labor, what unions was it composed of, and what were its goals?

Your Answer _____

_____

Q–383

Why did the influx of immigrants weaken the bargaining position of the early labor union?

Your Answer _____

_____

Q–384

True or False: After 1650, British authorities believed that the American colonists should have unregulated trade restrictions.

Your Answer _____

_____

Correct Answers

A–382

1) Samuel Gompers and Adolph Strasser
2) Craft unions
3) Higher wages, shorter hours, and improved safety conditions

A–383

Immigrants were willing to work for low wages and provided an available labor supply.

A–384

False. British authorities believed that American trade should be regulated for the benefit of the mother country.

Questions

Q–385

When was the Twenty-second Amendment to the Constitution ratified? What did it do?

Your Answer _____

_____

Q–386

What was the purpose of the Federal Trade Commission?

Your Answer _____

_____

Q–387

What was the Military Reconstruction Act of 1866?

Your Answer _____

_____

Correct Answers

A–385

1) 1951
2) The amendment limited the president to two terms.

A–386

To investigate unfair business practices

A–387

The Military Reconstruction Act of 1866 divided the South into five military districts to be ruled by military governors.

Questions

Q–388

What was controversial about 1928 Democratic presidential nominee Alfred Smith?

Your Answer _____

Q–389

What was significant about the Democrats nominating President Franklin Roosevelt for re-election in 1940?

Your Answer _____

Q–390

How did John F. Kennedy defuse the issue of his Catholicism during the 1960 campaign?

Your Answer _____

Correct Answers

A–388

He was Catholic and against Prohibition.

A–389

Since Roosevelt was being nominated for a third term, it broke with a tradition that had existed since the time of Washington that presidents would only serve two terms.

A–390

He told a gathering of Protestant ministers that he accepted separation of church and state and that Catholic leaders would not tell him how to act as president.

Questions

Why did President Andrew Jackson issue the Specie Circular?

Your Answer _____

_____

Why did a southern legislator remark "Cotton is King" in the antebellum period ?

Your Answer _____

_____

What was the major business trend during the 1920s?

Your Answer _____

_____

Correct Answers

A–391

He wanted to slow down the inflationary spiral, and this required that public land be paid for in hard money, not paper money or credit.

A–392

By 1860, cotton accounted for two-thirds of the value of U.S. exports.

A–393

The trend toward corporate consolidation

Questions

Q-394

What was a popular critique of corporate culture in the 1950s?

Your Answer _____

Q-395

What means of transportation were popular on the rivers and seas in the 1850s?

Your Answer _____

Q-396

What was the patroon system?

Your Answer _____

Correct Answers

A–394

That such environments encouraged the managerial personality and corporate cooperation rather than individualism

A–395

1) Steamboats
2) Clipper ships

A–396

To keep the colony of New Netherlands supplied with food, the Dutch devised the patroon system, which would award large landed estates to men who transported at least fifty families to the colony. These transported families would work as tenant farmers on the estate of the person who transported them.

Questions

Q–397

What was the Truman Doctrine? In what two countries was it first invoked?

Your Answer _____

Q–398

Why did the feminist movement suffer because of its link with the abolitionists?

Your Answer _____

Q–399

Who pioneered the mass-produced housing development in the 1950s?

Your Answer _____

Correct Answers

A–397

1) The Truman Doctrine stated that the United States must support free peoples who existed under Communist domination.
2) The doctrine was first invoked when the United States gave military and economic aid to Greece and Turkey in 1947.

A–398

Feminism was considered of secondary importance to the abolitionist cause.

A–399

William Levitt

Questions

Q–400

What was the only issue that united most Protestants in the 1920s?

Your Answer _____

_____

Q–401

What was the "Gospel of Wealth"?

Your Answer _____

_____

Q–402

Who were the "carpetbaggers"?

Your Answer _____

_____

Correct Answers

A–400

Support for Prohibition

A–401

A belief held by rich people that wealth was a gift from God given to a select few

A–402

Northerners who came to the South to take part in Reconstruction governments after the Civil War.

Questions

Q–403

What brought about the rise of the nativist movement during the late 1840s and early 1850s?

Your Answer _____

Q–404

Which groups supported the Federalists?

Your Answer _____

Q–405

What were *encomiendas*?

Your Answer _____

Correct Answers

A–403

The alarm of native-born Americans over the rising tide of German and Irish immigration

A–404

Business and financial groups in commercial centers of the Northeast and the port cities of the South

A–405

Encomiendas were large manors or estates with Indian slaves. They were developed to reward successful conquistadors and help the conquistadors deal with labor shortages.

Questions

Q–406

What were the two important economic initiatives made by President Richard Nixon in 1971?

Your Answer _____

_____

Q–407

What were the economic results of World War I in Europe?

Your Answer _____

_____

Q–408

How did President Eisenhower describe his legislative program?

Your Answer _____

_____

Correct Answers

A–406

Nixon announced a ninety-day price and wage freeze, and he took the United States off the gold standard.

A–407

Victorious and defeated nations all were in great debt, economies were devastated and took years to rebuild.

A–408

"Dynamic Conservatism"

Questions

Q–409

What was the name of the Bull Moose Party's platform in 1912? What were its major provisions?

Your Answer _____

_____

Q–410

What was the Tenure of Office Act?

Your Answer _____

_____

Q–411

Why did President Jackson, Henry Clay of Kentucky, and much of Congress not want to admit Texas into the Union when they first applied?

Your Answer _____

_____

Correct Answers

A–409

1) The New Nationalism
2) Federal old age; unemployment; accident insurance; eight-hour workdays; women's suffrage; abolition of child labor; and expanded public health services

A–410

The Tenure of Office Act was passed after the Civil War and established that federal officials whose appointment required Senate approval could not be removed from office without the Senate's consent. Congress passed the law in order to prevent President Andrew Johnson from dismissing any of his cabinet members, specifically Secretary of War Edwin M. Stanton.

A–411

Texas's admittance would upset the sectional balance and stir up the slavery issue. Also, Mexico threatened war if the United States annexed Texas.

Questions

Q–412

List four actions taken by the Jefferson administration that reversed former Federalist policies.

Your Answer _____

_____

Q–413

Who has been called the "father of the Constitution"?

Your Answer _____

_____

Q–414

Whose solo flight across the Atlantic in 1927 captured the world's imagination and made people feel that anything was possible?

Your Answer _____

_____

Correct Answers

A–412

1) Suspended enforcement of the Alien and Sedition Acts
2) Reduced the size of the federal bureaucracy
3) Repealed excise taxes
4) Reduced the size of the army

A–413

James Madison

A–414

Charles Lindbergh

Questions

Q–415

What happened in Little Rock, Arkansas, in 1957 concerning race relations?

Your Answer _____

_____

Q–416

What did the Niagara Movement want the federal government to do?

Your Answer _____

_____

Q–417

How did Congress respond when President Andrew Johnson fired his secretary of war, Edwin M. Stanton, from his cabinet?

Your Answer _____

_____

Correct Answers

A–415

President Dwight D. Eisenhower sent 10,000 National Guardsmen and 1,000 paratroopers to control mobs and enable blacks to enroll in Central High School.

A–416

Pass laws to protect racial equality and full rights of citizenship for African Americans

A–417

The House of Representatives impeached Johnson, and the Senate came within one vote of removing him from office.

Questions

Q–418

What were two reasons for the disintegration of the Whig Party during the 1850s?

Your Answer _____

_____

Q–419

How did John Adams guarantee continuation of Federalist policies after his presidency?

Your Answer _____

_____

Q–420

Which famous Federalist led the fight for ratification of the Constitution in New York?

Your Answer _____

_____

Correct Answers

A–418

1) The issue of slavery, which divided the party along North-South lines
2) The nativist movement

A–419

By filling judiciary positions, many newly created, with party supporters such as John Marshall. Many of these appointments occurred right at the end of his presidency and are thus referred to as "midnight judges."

A–420

Alexander Hamilton

Questions

Q–421

What was the first representative assembly in the New World?

Your Answer _____

_____

Q–422

Why was President Franklin D. Roosevelt reluctant to support antilynching legislation?

Your Answer _____

_____

Q–423

What was the purpose of the Tuskegee Institute?

Your Answer _____

_____

Correct Answers

A–421

The House of Burgesses

A–422

He was fearful of alienating the southern wing of the Democratic Party.

A–423

To provide teaching and vocational education for African Americans

Questions

Q–424

What was the Anti-Imperialist League?

Your Answer _____

_____

Q–425

What was the Ku Klux Klan and what was its purpose?

Your Answer _____

_____

Q–426

How was the public mood affected by the First World War?

Your Answer _____

_____

Correct Answers

A–424

The Anti-Imperialist League was an organization of Americans who opposed the United States's creating colonies out of territories it had captured from Spain.

A–425

The Ku Klux Klan was an organization formed by southerners to protect their racial traditions of segregation and white supremacy. They used violence to try to prevent blacks and white Republicans from voting.

A–426

A number of volunteer organizations sprang up around the country to search for draft dodgers, enforce the sale of bonds, and report any opinion or conversation considered suspicious. Organizations such as the American Protective League publicly humiliated people accused of not buying war bonds and persecuted, beat, and sometimes killed people of German descent.

Questions

Q–427

What conditions did President Andrew Johnson place on southern states before they could rejoin the Union?

Your Answer _____

Q–428

What famous saying is associated with President Calvin Coolidge?

Your Answer _____

Q–429

What did the Interstate Commerce Act of 1887 create?

Your Answer _____

Correct Answers

A–427

He required them to ratify the Thirteenth Amendment, repudiate Confederate debts, renounce secession, and give the vote to blacks.

A–428

"The business of the United States is business."

A–429

The Interstate Commerce Act of 1887 set up a commission to oversee fair railway rates, prohibit rebates, end discriminatory practices, and require annual financial reports from railroads.

Questions

Q–430

What policies did the Populist Party advocate?

Your Answer _____

_____

Q–431

What three things did the Compromise of 1850 give the South?

Your Answer _____

_____

Q–432

What two provisions about slavery did southern senators add to the original Kansas-Nebraska Act?

Your Answer _____

_____

Correct Answers

A–430

1) Coinage of silver at the ratio of 16 to 1
2) An eight-hour workday
3) The abolition of private armies used to break strikes
4) Direct election of senators
5) The right of initiative and referendum
6) The secret ballot
7) A graduated income tax

A–431

1) A tougher Fugitive Slave Law
2) Continuation of slavery in the District of Columbia
3) An agreement that Congress would have no jurisdiction over the interstate slave trade

A–432

The Missouri Compromise as it applied to Kansas and Nebraska was repealed, and the status of slavery in the two territories was to be decided by popular sovereignty.

Questions

Q–433

What was the Lecompton Constitution?

Your Answer _____

Q–434

What was Senator John Crittenden's proposal to preserve the Union?

Your Answer _____

Q–435

What was the Wade-Davis Bill?

Your Answer _____

Correct Answers

A–433

The Lecompton Constitution was a pro-slavery constitution for Kansas that was written by a fraudulent constitutional convention.

A–434

He proposed an extension of the Missouri Compromise line to the Pacific and prohibition of federal interference with slavery where it already existed. It was defeated due to President Lincoln's stance against the spread of slavery.

A–435

The Wade-Davis Bill stated that a loyal state government could be established if a majority of voters swore they had never been disloyal to the Union. President Lincoln "pocket vetoed" the bill.

Questions

Q–436

How did Congress respond to the refusal of southern states to ratify the Thirteenth Amendment, which would give the vote to blacks?

Your Answer _____

_____

Q–437

What happened to James A. Garfield soon after his election as president?

Your Answer _____

_____

Q–438

In what industry did the factory system in the United States start?

Your Answer _____

_____

Correct Answers

A–436

Congress passed a Civil Rights Act and extended the powers of the Freedman's Bureau.

A–437

A disappointed patronage seeker named Charles Guiteau assassinated him.

A–438

The textile industry

Questions

What explains the appeal of Governor George Wallace in the 1968 presidential election?

Your Answer _____

What was the Federal Emergency Relief Act? How was it administered?

Your Answer _____

What did the Seventeenth Amendment provide for?

Your Answer _____

Correct Answers

A–439

Fears generated by protestors, black militants, and an expanding bureaucracy

A–440

1) This law, passed in the first one hundred days of the Roosevelt administration, appropriated $500 million for aid to the poor to be distributed by state and local governments.
2) It was administered by the Federal Emergency Relief Administration.

A–441

The Seventeenth Amendment provided for the direct election of U.S. senators after 1913.

Questions

Q–442

Why did southern states vote to ratify the Fifteenth Amendment?

Your Answer _____

_____

Q–443

What was the "Kitchen Cabinet"?

Your Answer _____

_____

Q–444

Who authored *Walden* and *Civil Disobedience*, rejected the repression of society, and preached civil disobedience to protest unjust laws?

Your Answer _____

_____

Correct Answers

A–442

They had no choice if they were to be readmitted to the Union.

A–443

The Kitchen Cabinet was a group of partisan supporters from whom President Andrew Jackson took counsel instead of relying on the advice of his appointed cabinet officers.

A–444

Henry David Thoreau

Questions

Q–445

What event was a catalyst for the gay rights movement in the late 1960's?

Your Answer _____

_____

Q–446

What scandals erupted during President Grant's administration? Why was it so corrupt?

Your Answer _____

_____

Q–447

What was the Homestead Strike of 1892?

Your Answer _____

_____

Correct Answers

A–445

A police raid in 1969 on the Stonewall Inn, a gay hangout in the Greenwich Village section of New York City

A–446

1) The Gould-Fisk gold scandal; Credit Mobilier scandal; Whiskey Ring; Belknap accepting bribes
2) Although Grant was an honest man, he was loyal and trusted dishonest people.

A–447

A strike by iron and steel workers against the Carnegie Corporation in which Andrew Carnegie hired strike-breaking Pinkerton security guards, which resulted in people on both sides being killed

Questions

Who became an increasingly important consumer group during the 1950s?

Your Answer _____

_____

How did the sexual revolution affect women's clothing in the 1920s?

Your Answer _____

_____

Who constantly threatened the economic security of free blacks living in the cities during the 1850s?

Your Answer _____

_____

Correct Answers

A–448

Teenagers

A–449

Women adopted less bulky clothing, wearing short skirts and sleeveless and low-cut dresses.

A–450

Newly arrived immigrants who were willing to work for the least desirable jobs for lower wages

Questions

Q–451

What was the fastest-growing region in the country during the first half of the nineteenth century?

Your Answer _____

Q–452

Apart from the English, which other groups immigrated to America during the early 1700s?

Your Answer _____

Q–453

Why were the Alien and Sedition Acts of 1798 passed?

Your Answer _____

Correct Answers

A–451

The West

A–452

Scots-Irish and Germans

A–453

To stifle actual or potential Democrat Republican opposition to the Federalist-controlled government during the "undeclared war" with France

Questions

Q–454

Henry Clay, John C. Calhoun, and other strong pro-war Congressmen became known as _____ _____.

Your Answer _____

Q–455

What did the Sherman Anti-Trust Act of 1890 provide?

Your Answer _____

Q–456

What areas of the country supported Thomas Jefferson and the Republicans?

Your Answer _____

Correct Answers

A–454

War Hawks

A–455

The Sherman Anti-Trust Act subjected trusts that controlled whole industries to federal prosecution if they were in restraint of trade.

A–456

The rural areas of the South and West

Questions

Q–457

During the mid- to late nineteenth century, what developments indicated that the American public was becoming more educated?

Your Answer _____

Q–458

Which British act imposed a tax on every piece of printed paper, from newspapers to legal documents, in the colonies?

Your Answer _____

Q–459

What happened at Lexington and Concord?

Your Answer _____

Correct Answers

A–457

A proliferation of newspapers and magazines and the springing up of new colleges indicated that the American public was becoming more educated.

A–458

The Stamp Act of 1765

A–459

The British marched to Concord to destroy a stockpile of colonial weapons. News of their march was spread by riders like Paul Revere and William Dawes. Minutemen—a select group of armed militia—were waiting for the British at Lexington. A shot was fired and eight Minutemen were killed. By the time the British arrived at Concord, all supplies had been moved.

Questions

Q–460

What territory was returned to Spain in the Treaty of Paris?

Your Answer _____

Q–461

What was the meaning of James K. Polk's presidential campaign slogan, "Fifty-four forty or fight"?

Your Answer _____

Q–462

What was the Bear Flag Revolt?

Your Answer _____

Correct Answers

A–460

Florida

A–461

The slogan meant that Polk favored American annexation of the Oregon country (up to the 54° 40′ north latitude line), which previously had been jointly occupied by the United States and Great Britain.

A–462

A revolt against the Mexican government by American settlers in California in the 1840's.

Questions

Q–463

Why did some people support the Mexican War while others opposed it?

Your Answer _____

_____

Q–464

Describe the Espionage and Sedition Acts.

Your Answer _____

_____

Q–465

What factor contributed to the increased number of strikes in 1919? In what city did the police strike? Why did public support for striking workers diminish?

Your Answer _____

_____

Correct Answers

A–463

Some people supported the war because they felt Mexico had provoked it, and it gave the United States an opportunity to spread freedom to oppressed people. Others opposed the war because they felt the United States provoked the war, or it was a war to spread slavery.

A–464

The Espionage Act of 1917 provided for fines and imprisonment for persons who made false statements that aided the enemy, incited rebellion in the military, or obstructed recruitment or the draft. The Sedition Act of May 1918 forbade any criticism of the government, flag, or uniform, even if there were not detrimental consequences.

A–465

1) The rapid postwar inflation contributed to the striking workers demand for higher wages.
2) Boston
3) The Communist Revolution of 1917 in Russia made many Americans fear violence and revolution by workers.

Questions

Q–466

What was the Stamp Act Congress?

Your Answer _____

_____

Q–467

How did many slaves survive the horrors of slavery?

Your Answer _____

_____

Q–468

What was the political result of the California gold rush of 1849?

Your Answer _____

_____

Correct Answers

A–466

The Stamp Act Congress consisted of delegates from nine colonies that met in 1765 and passed moderate resolutions against the Stamp Act, asserting that Americans could not be taxed without representation.

A–467

They developed a distinctive network of tradition and interdependence.

A–468

California's population soared from 14,000 to 100,000 in one year, and since there was no territorial government, California sought immediate admission as a state.

Questions

Q–469

What was the major issue that President Martin Van Buren had to deal with during his administration?

Your Answer _____

_____

Q–470

What was the Judiciary Act of 1789?

Your Answer _____

_____

Q–471

What is the Electoral College?

Your Answer _____

_____

Correct Answers

A–469

The financial chaos and resulting depression (1837) left by the demise of the Second National Bank

A–470

The Judiciary Act of 1789 provided for a federal court system and a Supreme Court consisting of six justices, and created jurisdictions for the federal courts.

A–471

The Electoral College is a body of electors from each state, based on the state's combined number of senators and representatives. Its function is to elect the president.

Questions

Q–472

What was the most popular form of music in the 1930s?

Your Answer _____

_____

Q–473

What issues did the women's rights movement of the 1830s and 1840s focus upon?

Your Answer _____

_____

Q–474

What was "the Great Compromise"? What plans did it incorporate?

Your Answer _____

_____

Correct Answers

A–472

Swing or big band music

A–473

Social and legal discrimination

A–474

The Great Compromise was the agreement reached at the Constitutional Convention of 1787 that established the federal government's bicameral legislature: a Senate in which each state was represented by two senators (New Jersey Plan), and a House of Representatives based on population (Virginia Plan).

Questions

Which nineteenth-century Hudson River School artist painted a wide array of American birds and animals?

Your Answer _____

What was the effect of radio on American culture?

Your Answer _____

Which branch has the power to impeach the president or other high government officials?

Your Answer _____

Correct Answers

A–475

John James Audubon

A–476

It tended to make Americans more uniform in their attitudes, taste, speech, and humor.

A–477

The legislative branch, or Congress

Questions

What was the Boxer Rebellion?

Your Answer _____

_____

How did "dollar diplomacy" differ from "big stick" diplomacy?

Your Answer _____

_____

What was the Sussex Pledge?

Your Answer _____

_____

Correct Answers

A–478

The Boxer Rebellion was a revolt by Chinese nationalists against foreign settlements in China and against the Manchu government for granting industrial concessions in China to foreign nations.

A–479

"Dollar diplomacy" emphasized economic development, while "big stick" diplomacy emphasized military and political intervention.

A–480

The Germans pledged to give adequate warning before sinking merchant and passenger ships and to provide for the safety of passengers and crew. The Sussex Pledge was prompted by the torpedoing of the French passenger steamer the *Sussex*, on March 24, 1916.

Questions

Q–481

What was the War Labor Board? How did World War I affect union membership?

Your Answer _____

Q–482

In addition to France, name two other countries that joined America in its war against Britain after 1776.

Your Answer _____

Q–483

What did the Declaratory Act of 1768 state?

Your Answer _____

Correct Answers

A–481

1) The War Labor Board was created on March 29, 1918, to prevent strikes and work stoppages in war industries.
2) Union membership doubled during the war from about 2.5 million to 5 million.

A–482

Holland and Spain

A–483

The Declaratory Act of 1768 claimed the power to tax or make laws for Americans in all cases.

Questions

Q–484

What famous young major of the Virginia militia was sent to western Pennsylvania to expel the French in the 1750's?

Your Answer _____

Q–485

In general, why did American colonists dislike the Navigation Acts?

Your Answer _____

Q–486

When did the Soviet Union launch *Sputnik*? What were some of the consequences in the United States?

Your Answer _____

Correct Answers

A–484

George Washington

A–485

The Navigation Acts increased the prices that Americans had to pay for British goods and lowered the prices that Americans received for the goods they produced.

A–486

1) October 4, 1957
2) The launch of the Sputnik satellite created fear that the United States was falling behind technologically, and as a result, in 1958 Congress established the National Aeronautics and Space Administration (NASA) to coordinate research and development, and passed the National Defense Education Act to provide grants and loans for education.

Questions

Q–487

What catastrophic event in 1986 damaged NASA's credibility?

Your Answer _____

Q–488

What is the purpose of the Securities and Exchange Commission?

Your Answer _____

Q–489

What did the Supreme Court decide in its 1973 *Roe v. Wade* decision?

Your Answer _____

Correct Answers

A–487

The explosion of the space shuttle *Challenger*

A–488

To supervise stock exchanges and to punish fraud in securities trading

A–489

Roe v. Wade legalized abortion during the first three months of pregnancy.

Questions

What two Supreme Court decisions stipulated that blacks must be allowed to attend integrated law schools?

Your Answer _____

_____

What policies regarding money did farm groups advocate during the 1870s and 1880s?

Your Answer _____

_____

What precedent was set by Chief Justice John Marshall in *Marbury v. Madison*?

Your Answer _____

_____

Correct Answers

A–490

Ada Lois Sipuel v. Board of Regents (1948) and *Sweatt v. Painter* (1950)

A–491

Currency inflation and the use of both gold and silver to back money

A–492

Marshall asserted the power of judicial review over federal legislation.

Questions

What is OPEC? How did it affect the United States in the 1970s?

Your Answer _____

_____

When was the Korean armistice signed? What was the war's outcome?

Your Answer _____

_____

What was the Good Neighbor Policy?

Your Answer _____

_____

Correct Answers

A–493

1) The Organization of Petroleum Exporting Countries (OPEC) is a cartel of oil-producing nations; its founding members are Venezuela, Saudi Arabia, Kuwait, Iraq, and Iran.
2) OPEC significantly raised oil prices in the early 1970s. This action doubled gas prices in the United States and raised inflation above 10 percent.

A–494

1) June 1953
2) Korea was divided along virtually the same boundary that had existed prior to the war. No military advantage had been gained by either side.

A–495

The Good Neighbor Policy was an attempt by President Franklin D. Roosevelt's administration to improve relations with Latin American nations.

Questions

Q–496

Who were the first men to walk on the moon? When?

Your Answer _____

Q–497

What did the Supreme Court declare in its *Brown v. Board of Education* decision?

Your Answer _____

Q–498

How did Chief Justice Marshall's decisions affect the balance of powers between the federal and state governments?

Your Answer _____

Correct Answers

A–496

1) Neil Armstrong and Edwin (Buzz) Aldrin
2) July 20, 1969

A–497

In 1954, the Court declared that separate educational facilities were inherently unequal and that states had to integrate with "all deliberate speed."

A–498

Marshall's decisions strengthened the federal and weakened the states' powers.

Questions

Q–499

What was the basis of President Jimmy Carter's foreign policy?

Your Answer _____

_____

Q–500

How was Jamestown saved?

Your Answer _____

_____

Correct Answers

A–499

Human rights considerations

A–500

Jamestown was ravaged by disease and famine in the first year of its establishment. When John Smith arrived, he required all those who wished to eat, to work. Later on, John Rolfe introduced better farming techniques for growing tobacco, which became the backbone of the Virginian economy.

Index

[Note: Numbers in the Index refer to question numbers.]

A

Abolitionist movement, 123, 398
Abortion, 262, 489
Ada Lois Sipuel v. *Board of Regents,* 490
Adams, John, 73, 181, 419
Adams, John Quincy, 265
Adams, Samuel, 102
Adams-Otis Treaty, 65
Adventures of Tom Sawyer (Twain), 78
Advertising, 168
Afghanistan
    Soviet invasion of, 67
African Americans
    Black Codes, 321
    immigrants and, 450
    Jim Crow laws, 138
    Ku Klux Klan and, 425
    Niagara Movement, 416
    Tuskegee Institute, 423
    voting, 362
    World War I and migration, 2
    in WW I, 329
Agrarian economy, 85
Agricultural Adjustment Act, 193
AIDS, 380
Airplane, 35, 414
Alamogordo, New Mexico, 296
Aldrin, Edwin, 496
Alger, Horatio, 51
Alien and Sedition Acts, 412, 453

America First Committee, 21
American Federation of Labor (AFL), 374, 382
American Protective League, 426
American Railway Union, 335
American Revolution, 33, 96, 245, 379, 459
Anti-Imperialist League, 424
Anti-Saloon League, 319
Antislavery movement, 251
Arizona, 294
Armstrong, Neil, 496
Articles of Confederation, 120, 274
Atlantic Charter, 344
Atomic bomb, 11, 295
Atomic chain reaction, 369
Audubon, John James, 475
Automobiles, 98, 153, 358
Aztec Empire, 349

B

Bacon, Nathaniel, 9
Bacon's Rebellion, 9
Balboa, Vasco Nunez de, 36
Banking, 217
Bank of the United States, 107
Baseball, 172
Bay of Pigs, 211
Bear Flag Revolt, 462
Bell, Alexander Graham, 64
Berlin Crisis, 32

[Note: Numbers in the Index refer to question numbers.]

Big band music, 472
Big stick diplomacy, 479
Bill of Rights, 266
Black Codes, 321
Bleeding Kansas, 6, 231
Bonus Army, 238
Boston, 465
Boston Massacre, 102
Boston Tea Party, 33
Boxer Rebellion, 478
Brain Trust, 305
Brown, John, 188, 231
Brown v. Board of Education,
    252, 497
Bull Moose Party, 409

C

Calhoun, John C., 119, 454
California, 322, 462, 468
Canada, 326
Carnegie, Andrew, 83, 447
Carnegie Corporation, 447
Carolina Colonies, 310
Carpetbaggers, 402
Carter, Jimmy, 67, 150, 499
Cartier, Jacques, 367
Carver, George Washington, 25
Castro, Fidel, 211
Catholics, 91, 314, 390
    immigrants, 60
Challenger, 487
Chavez, Cesar, 145
Cherokee, 24
Chesapeake Bay colony, 41, 311
Chicago, 178, 186
Chicago World's Fair, 141
Child Labor Act, 81
China, 94, 115, 157, 297
Chinese immigrants, 254

Cholera, 292
Churchill, Winston, 344
Cities
    standard of living, 56
Civil Disobedience (Thoreau), 444
Civilian Conservation Corps, 177
Civil Rights Act, 160, 331, 436
Civil Rights Commission, 331
Civil rights movement, 175, 176,
    267
Civil War
    Bleeding Kansas, 6
    Britain and France, 95
    copperheads, 5
    draft, 371
    factories and, 377
    farmers during, 117
    paying for, 39
    prices during, 69
    reconstruction, 72
    succession, 325
Clark, William, 49
Clay, Henry, 411, 454
Clearing and planting farming,
    50
Clermont, 148
Cleveland, Grover, 298, 333
Coal power, 86
Coal strike, 202
Coercive Acts, 96, 213, 244
Colleges, 323, 457
Colonies, early American
    British control of, 30
    Chesapeake Bay, 41
    indentured servants, 42
    Jamestown, 43
    Navigation Acts, 485
    New England, 10, 41
    patroon system, 396
    Stamp Act, 458, 466

trade restrictions and, 384
Columbus, Christopher, 26
Common Sense (Paine), 52
Communism, 115
Communist Revolution, 465
Compromise of 1850, 195, 431
Compromise of 1877, 139
Concord, 459
Confederate States of America, 31
Congress, 477
Congress of Industrial Organizations (CIO), 374
Conquistadores, 34
Conservation, 48
Constitution, U.S., 120, 121, 364, 413, 474
Constitutional Convention, 474
Consumers, 448
Continental Congress, 351
Coolidge, Calvin, 428
Copperheads, 5
Corporations, 393, 394
Cortes, Hernando, 349
Cotton, 299, 334, 392
Cotton gin, 132
Court packing, 288
Crack cocaine, 112
Credit Mobilier scandal, 446
Crime of '73, 80
Crittenden, John, 434
Cuba, 155, 211

D

Davis, Jefferson, 31
Dawes, William, 459
D-Day, 68
Debs, Eugene, 335
de Champlain, Samuel, 350

Declaration of Independence, 327
Declaratory Act, 483
Democratic Party, 136
Democrat Republicans, 107, 453
Depression of 1819, 280
Depression of 1893, 241, 319
Détente, 210
Dickinson, John, 248
Dix, Dorothea, 220
Dixiecrat Party, 136
Dollar diplomacy, 479
Domino theory, 156
Douglas, Stephen, 89, 105
Douglass, Frederick, 221
Dred Scott decision, 22, 89
DuBois, W.E.B., 128
Dynamic Conservatism, 408

E

Edison, Thomas, 300
Education, 457, 497
  for women, 129
Eisenhower, Dwight, 211, 408, 415
Electoral College, 29, 471
Emancipation Proclamation, 275
Embargo Act, 208
Encomiendas, 405
Enlightenment, 232, 250
Equal Employment Opportunity Commission, 160
Equal Rights Amendment, 262
Erie Canal, 189
Espionage Act, 464

F

Factories, 438
Fair Deal Program, 40

Fair Employment Practice
  Committee, 224
Fall, Albert B., 264
Farmers' Alliances, 179
Farming, 50, 85, 117, 152, 179,
  193, 215, 269, 299, 359,
  375, 491, 500
Federal Emergency Relief Act, 440
Federal Housing Administration
  (FHA), 285
Federalist Papers, 171
Federalists, 404, 419, 420
Federal Reserve Act, 62, 217
Federal Reserve Notes, 62
Federal Reserve System, 62, 147,
  260
Federal Trade Commission, 386
Federal Trade Commission Act,
  225
Feminine Mystique, The
  (Friedan), 122
Feminist movement, 398
Fermi, Enrico, 369
Fifteenth Amendment, 362, 442
First Amendment, 121
First Continental Congress, 244
First New Deal, 71
Florida, 65, 110, 460
Flour milling, 261
Force Bill, 119
Ford, Gerald, 360
Ford, Henry, 98, 153
Fourteenth Amendment, 247
France, 45, 46, 47, 95, 181, 200,
  209, 216, 482
Franklin, Benjamin, 108
Freedman's Bureau, 436
Freedom Riders, 267
Freeport Doctrine, 89
Free Speech Movement, 249

Friedan, Betty, 122
Fugitive Slave Act, 287, 431
Fulton, Robert, 148
Fur trade, 200

G

Gadsden Purchase, 294
Garfield, James, 437
Garrison, William Lloyd, 123
Garvey, Marcus, 126
Gay rights movement, 445
German immigrants, 314, 403,
  452
Germany, 93, 291, 372, 373
Ghent, Treaty of, 378
Gibbons v. Ogden, 342
GI Bill, 233
Gilded Age, 218
Glorious Revolution, 242
Gold, 290, 468, 491
Gold standard, 406
Gompers, Samuel, 382
Good Neighbor Policy, 495
Gorbachev, Mikhail, 343
Gospel of Wealth, 401
Gould-Fisk gold scandal, 446
Grant, Ulysses S., 194, 446
Great Awakening, 257, 323
Great Britain, 95, 209, 270, 357
Great Compromise, 474
Great Depression
  Civilian Conservation Corps,
    177
  economic effects of, 144
  Hoovervilles, 167
  New Deal, 71, 201
  stock market crash and, 38
  Works Progress Administration
    (WPA), 55

Greece, 397
Greenback-Labor Party, 240
Greenbacks, 84, 191
Guiteau, Charles, 437

H

Hamilton, Alexander, 107, 171, 420
Harper's Ferry, 188
Harrison, William Henry, 352
Hartford Convention, 363
Hawley-Smoot Tariff, 116
Hayes, Rutherford B., 82, 139
Hayne, Robert, 170
Headright system, 42
Holland, 272, 482
Homestead Strike, 447
Hoover, Herbert, 37, 238
Hoovervilles, 167
House of Burgesses, 421
Howe, Elias, 293
Hudson River School, 475
Huerto, Victoriano, 206
Hutchinson, Thomas, 33

I

Immigrant/immigration
  in 1870s and 1880s, 4
  Catholic, 314
  Chinese, 254
  free blacks and, 450
  German, 314, 403, 452
  Irish, 7, 254, 314, 403
  nativist movement, 403
  old vs. new movement, 187
  political support and, 255
  Scots-Irish, 313, 452
  settlement houses, 317

unions and, 383
Income tax, 39, 222
Indentured servants, 9, 42
Indian Reorganization Act, 92
Industrial Revolution, 104
Industrial Workers of the World, 14, 198
Interstate Commerce Act, 429
Intolerable Acts, 213
Iraq, 204
Irish immigrants, 7, 254, 314, 403
Iron, 261
Ironclad ship, 63

J

Jackson, Andrew, 61, 119, 154, 391, 411, 443
Jacksonian era, 106, 196
Jamestown, Virginia, 43, 500
Japan, 23, 94, 114, 277, 291, 355
Japanese-American internment camps, 184
Jay, John, 171
Jazz Age, 347
Jefferson, Thomas, 73, 107, 327, 412, 455
Jim Crow laws, 138
Johnson, Andrew, 410, 417, 427
Jones, John Paul, 149
Jones, Mary Harris, 14
Judiciary Act, 470

K

Kansas, 6, 315
Kansas-Nebraska Act, 432
Kellogg-Briand Pact, 205
Kennedy, John F., 211, 366, 390

Kent State University, 130
Kentucky Resolve, 73
King, Martin Luther, Jr., 175
Kissinger, Henry, 157
Kitchen Cabinet, 443
Knights of Labor, 258
Know-Nothings, 236
Korea, 494
Korematsu v. United States, 184
Ku Klux Klan, 253, 425
Kuwait, 204

L

Lancastrian System, 336
Lecompton Constitution, 433
Lend-Lease assistance, 373
Letters from a Farmer in
    Pennsylvania, 301
Levitt, William, 399
Lewis, Meriwether, 49
Lexington, 459
Liberator, The, 123
Lincoln, Abraham, 89, 105, 226,
    325, 354, 434, 435
Lincoln-Douglass debates, 105
Lindbergh, Charles, 414
Line of Demarcation, 271
Little Rock, Arkansas, 415
Locke, John, 197
Lowell System, 304
Lusitania, 302
Luther, Martin, 97

M

MacArthur, Douglas, 238
Macon's Bill, 113
Madison, James, 73, 107, 171, 413
Maine, 90

Maine, 337
Manhattan Project, 11
Manifest destiny, 13
Mao Tse-tung, 115
Marbury v. *Madison,* 492
March on Washington, 175
Marshall, John, 342, 419, 492, 498
Maryland, 91
Mayflower Compact, 19
McCormick, Cyrus, 259
McKinley, William, 137
McKinley Tariff, 376
Medicare Act, 16
Meredith, James, 366
Mexican War, 207, 463
Mexico, 206, 462
Midnight judges, 419
Migration
    during World War I, 2
Military Reconstruction Act, 387
Minutemen, 459
Mississippi, 366
Mississippi River, 110, 245
Missouri, 90
Missouri Compromise, 90, 432, 434
Money, 84, 191, 274, 289, 290,
    406, 491
Monopolies, 235, 359
Monroe Doctrine, 70, 182
Moral majority movement, 262
Morse, Samuel, 368
Moscow Olympics, 67
Moving assembly line, 98
Muckrakers, 127
Mugwumps, 333

N

NAFTA, 229
Napoleonic Wars, 45

National Aeronautics and Space Administration (NASA), 486, 487
National Association for the Advancement of Colored People (NAACP), 176
National Bank, 61
National Conservation Commission, 48
National Defense Education Act, 486
National Grange, 179
National Industrial Recovery Act, 381
National Labor Relations Board (NLRB), 151
National Labor Union, 258
National Parks, 48
National Republicans, 265
National Road, 180
Native Americans, 154, 200, 212, 243, 345
　French and, 47
　Indian Reorganization Act, 92
　Trail of Tears, 24
Nativist movement, 403, 418
Navigation Acts, 485
Navy, U.S., 149
New Deal, 40, 71, 142, 201
New England colony, 10, 41, 192
New Freedom, 88
New imperialism, 282
New Mexico, 294
New Nationalism, 409
New Orleans, 148
Newspapers, 457
New York City, 186
New York Free School, 336
Niagara Movement, 128, 416
Nineteenth Amendment, 246

Nixon, Richard, 87, 157, 210, 360, 406
Non-Intercourse Act, 113
North Star, 221
Northwest Passage, 367
Nuclear Test Ban Treaty, 214

O

OPEC, 493
Open Door Policy, 297
Operation Desert Shield, 204
Operation Desert Storm, 204
Ordinance of Nullification, 119
Oregon Fever, 281
Oregon Trail, 256
Oregon Treaty, 357
Organization of Petroleum Exporting Countries (OPEC), 493
Organized crime, 76

P

Paine, Thomas, 52
Panama Canal, 277, 295
Panic of 1873, 134
Panic of 1907, 217
Paris, Treaty of, 245, 326, 460
Parks, Rosa, 53
Patroon system, 396
Peninsulares, 308
Perkins, Frances, 234
Perry, Matthew, 23
Philadelphia, 186
Pilgrims, 19
Pinckney Treaty, 110
Plantation system, 334
Planter class, 316
Poe, Edgar Allan, 125

Political machines, 161
Polk, James, 279, 353, 461
Pontiac, 243
Poor Richard's Almanac
    (Franklin), 108
Populist Party, 430
Portsmouth, Treaty of, 114
Portugal, 103, 271
Pottawatomie Massacre, 231
Proclamation of 1763, 324
Progressive Era, 118
Progressive Party, 136
Prohibition, 76, 230, 400
Prosser, Gabriel, 239
Protestant Reformation, 97
Protestants
    temperance movement, 60
Public Works Administration,
    348
Puget Sound, 270
Pure Food and Drug Act, 286
Puritans, 10

Q

Quakers, 312
Quartering Act, 227
Quebec, 350
Quebec Act, 213

R

Race Riots of 1919, 178
Radio, 476
Railroads, 12, 82, 219, 284, 289
Randolph, A. Philip, 224
"Raven, The" (Poe), 125
Reagan, Ronald, 146
Realism, 318
Reaper, 259

Reconstruction, 72, 139, 402
Reconstruction Finance
    Corporation (RFC), 278
Religious Toleration, Act of, 91
Republican Party, 27, 79, 236
Revere, Paul, 459
Robber barons, 28
Rockefeller, John D., 135
Roe v. *Wade,* 489
Rolfe, John, 500
Romantic movement, 173, 318
Roosevelt, Franklin D., 184, 224,
    234, 263, 288, 305, 344,
    389, 422, 495
Roosevelt, Theodore, 48, 79, 94,
    114, 118, 137, 155, 202,
    235
Roosevelt Corollary, 182
Rosenberg, Ethel, 199
Rosenberg, Julius, 199
Rural Electrification
    Administration (REA),
    320
Russo-Japanese War, 114
Ruth, Babe, 172

S

Sacco, 140
Sack of Lawrence, 231
St. Lawrence River, 216, 367
Salem witch trials, 8
SALT (Strategic Arms Limitation
    Treaty) agreement, 44, 67
Saratoga, New York, 46
Saudi Arabia, 204
Savio, Mario, 249
Schools, 332, 336, 340
Scopes, John Thomas, 203
Scopes trial, 203

Scots-Irish immigrants, 313, 452
Second Continental Congress, 248
Second Great Awakening, 100
Second National Bank, 469
Securities and Exchange Commission, 488
Sedition Act, 464
Selective Service and Training Act, 361
Seneca Falls, New York, 164
Serbia, 183
Settlement houses, 317
Seventeenth Amendment, 441
Seven Years War, 209
Sewing machine, 293
Sexual revolution, 449
Shays, Daniel, 101
Shays' Rebellion, 101, 159
Sherman Anti-Trust Act, 455
Sherman Silver Purchase Act, 290
Ships, 63, 99, 148, 395
Silver, 80, 290, 491
Sixteenth Amendment, 222
Slaves/slavery
  antislavery movement, 251
  Compromise of 1850, 195, 431
  Dred Scott decision, 22
  Emancipation Proclamation, 275
  Fugitive Slave Act, 287
  importation of, 77
  Kansas-Nebraska Act, 432
  Missouri Compromise, 432, 434
  ownership of, 59
  Republican Party, 236
  survival skills, 467
  Three-Fifths Compromise, 330

in towns, 339
Smith, Alfred, 388
Smith, John, 500
Social Darwinism, 58
Social gospel, 3
Social Security, 40, 185
South
  cotton and, 392
  economy of, 85
  farming, 215
  industries in, 133
  manufacturing industries, 261
  plantation system, 334
  planter class, 316
  prices during Civil War, 69
  public schools, 340
  reconstruction, 72
  slave ownership, 59
South Carolina, 370
Soviet Union, 157, 343, 356, 486
  Berlin Crisis, 32
  German invasion of, 373
  invasion of Afghanistan, 67
Spain, 103, 110, 158, 271, 308, 482
Specie Circular, 391
Specie Redemption Act, 191
Sputnik, 486
Square deal, 118
Stamp Act, 273, 458, 466
Standard Oil Company, 135
Stanton, Edwin M., 410, 417
Steamboat, 148, 395
Steel industry, 83, 133
Stock market, 38, 488
Stonewall Inn, 445
Stowe, Harriet Beecher, 20
Strasser, Adolph, 382
Strikes, 465, 481
Submarine Crisis of 1915, 302

[Note: Numbers in the Index refer to question numbers.]

Submarine warfare, 93, 302, 480
Suburbs, 169
Sugar, 299
Sumter, Fort, 226
Sunbelt states, 75
Supply-side economics, 27
Supreme Court, 288, 470, 489, 490, 497
Sussex Pledge, 480
Sweatt v. *Painter,* 490
Swing music, 472

T

Taft, William Howard, 79
Taft-Hartley Act, 111
Tariff of Abomination, 109
Teapot Dome Scandal, 264
Tecumseh, 212, 352
Teenagers, 448
Telegraph, 368
Telephone, 64
Television, 338
Temperance movement, 60
Tennessee Valley Authority (TVA), 1
Tenure of Office Act, 410
Texas, 411
Textile industry, 133, 261, 438
Thirteenth Amendment, 427, 436
Thoreau, Henry David, 444
Three-Fifths Compromise, 330
Thresher, 259
Thurmond, Strom, 136
Tobacco, 133
Tokyo Bay, 23
Tordesillas, Treaty of, 103
Trade deficits, 291
Trail of Tears, 24
Transcendentalists, 124, 365

Triple Alliance, 328
Triple Entente, 328
Truman, Harry S., 40, 54, 136
Truman Doctrine, 397
Trusts, 15, 235
Turkey, 397
Turner, Nat, 239
Tuskegee Institute, 25, 268, 423
Twain, Mark, 78
Twenty-second Amendment, 385
Typhoid fever, 292
Typhus, 292

U

Uncle Tom's Cabin (Stowe), 20
Underground Railroad, 163
Unemployment, 201, 241
Unions, 111, 145, 146, 190, 198, 202, 258, 374, 382, 383, 481
United Nations, 66

V

Van Buren, Martin, 469
Vanzetti, 140
Versailles Treaty, 372
Vesey, Denmark, 239
Vespucci, Amerigo, 26
Veto power, 307
Vietnam War, 156, 174
Virginia, 309
Virginia Resolve, 73
Voting, 246, 362

W

Wade-Davis Bill, 435
Wagner Act, 151

[Note: Numbers in the Index refer to question numbers.]

Walden (Thoreau), 444
Wallace, George, 439
Wallace, Henry, 136
War Hawks, 454
War Industries Board, 276
War Labor Board, 481
Washington, Booker T., 268
Washington, George, 18, 484
Watergate, 87
Waving bloody shirt, 223
Webster, Daniel, 170
Webster-Ashburton Treaty, 346
Webster-Hayne Debate, 170
Whigs, 236, 418
Whiskey Rebellion, 18
Whiskey Ring, 446
White Citizens' Council, 252
White flight, 166
Whitney, Eli, 132
Wilson, Woodrow, 17, 88, 206,
    302
Wobblies, 14, 198
Women
    after WW II, 165
    education and, 129
    feminist movement, 398
    homemaking skills, 341
    sexual revolution and clothing,
        449

voting, 246
women's rights movement, 74,
    162, 164, 473
Works Progress Administration
    (WPA), 55
World War I
    African Americans in, 329
    American decision to join, 93
    American neutrality, 303
    consequences for blacks and
        minorities, 2
    economic results of, 407
    prohibition and, 230
    public mood and, 426
World War II, 21, 68
Wright brothers, 35

XYZ Affair, 181

Yalta Conference, 356
Yellow journalism, 57

Zimmerman telegram, 93